Date Due

APR 3 1978 1979	NOV 2 0 1979		
JAN 1 9 1982			

MALCOI

FORM 109

The Sixties

Wyndham Lewis in Canada, with an Introduction by Julian Symons

MALCOLM LOWRY:
THE MAN AND HIS WORK

edited by

GEORGE WOODCOCK

University of British Columbia Press
Vancouver

MALCOLM LOWRY: THE MAN AND HIS WORK

International Standard Book Number: 7748-0006-2

Printed in Canada by
The Morriss Printing Company Ltd.
Victoria, British Columbia

CONTENTS

INTERLUDE

BIOGRAPHICAL NOTE

IN 1909 MALCOLM LOWRY — Malcolm Boden Lowry to give him his full name — was born in one of the dormitory towns of the Wirral on the south side of the Mersey where Liverpool business men lived in the early years of the century; his father was a cotton broker in the city. After the customary English middle-class experience of being wrenched from his family at the age of seven to attend boarding school, he embarked in his late teens on a freighter bound for the Far East. The experience provided material for his first novel *Ultramarine*. After several voyages, which enabled him to see much of the Pacific, he returned to England in 1929; on the way he had already met the American poet Conrad Aiken, who was to become his literary guru.

After graduating at Cambridge, Lowry travelled in Spain (a foretaste of Mexico), lived for a while in France and in the London bohemian world, and went to Hollywood, where he wrote film scripts and married his first wife Jan. With her he moved to Cuernavaca in Mexico, and there started work on *Under the Volcano*, which was not completed until 1947, long after he and Jan had been divorced. After their parting, Lowry moved north in 1939 to British Columbia, where he settled in the now vanished shack colony at Dollarton on Burrard Inlet. In 1940 he married Margerie Bonner, a film star and writer of mystery stories from Hollywood. On and off, with trips to Mexico, Europe and to Niagara-on-the-Lake, he lived at Dollarton until 1954, writing continually, publishing little, but leaving the vast mass of occasionally finished but more often incomplete works which have been appearing since his death and which are discussed in the following essays and listed in the bibliography. Lowry left Dollarton in 1954, and lived for a while in Sicily. He found it unsympathetic, and moved to England, where in 1957, in the village of Ripe, he died, as the coroner found, "of misadventure". He had expressed his intent of returning to Canada.

The only books to be published by Lowry during his life were *Ultramarine* and *Under the Volcano*; his inability to complete any work, which reached pathological dimensions in his later years, made him the despair of publishers, and most of his now considerable list of books appeared posthumously, prepared for publication by others, notably his widow, Margerie Bonner Lowry, and his friend and fellow poet, Earle Birney.

NOTE ON THE TEXT

MALCOLM LOWRY's "Some Poems" appeared in *Canadian Literature* 8, his "Preface to a Novel" in *Canadian Literature* 9, and "Two Letters" in *Canadian Literature* 44. We acknowledge with thanks the permission of Mrs. Margerie Lowry to reprint these and of Dr. Earle Birney to reprint his Preface to "Some Poems".

William McConnell's "Recollections of Malcolm Lowry" appeared in *Canadian Literature* 7. Robert B. Heilman's "The Possessed Artist and the Ailing Soul", George Woodcock's "Under Seymour Mountain", Conrad Aiken's "Malcolm Lowry: A Note", and Downie Kirk's "More than Music" appeared in *Canadian Literature* 8. Anthony R. Kilgallin's "Faust and Under the Volcano" appeared in *Canadian Literature* 26. Geoffrey Durrant's "Death in Life", David Benham's "Lowry's Purgatory", W. H. New's "Lowry's Reading", Paul G. Tiessen's "Malcolm Lowry and the Cinema" and Perle Epstein's "Swinging the Maelstrom", appeared in *Canadian Literature* 44. George Woodcock's "Art and the Writer's Mirror" appeared in his volume of essays, *Odysseus Ever Returning* (McClelland & Stewart), as did, in slightly different form, four paragraphs of his Introduction.

Matthew Corrigan's "The Writer as Consciousness", Anthony R. Kilgallin's "The Long Voyage Home", Hilda Thomas's "Lowry's Letters" and Maurice J. Carey's "Life with Malcolm Lowry" are all previously unpublished. We gratefully acknowledge the permission of all these authors to print their pieces, and wish to thank Mrs. Downie Kirk for permission to reprint the article by her late husband.

Each article has been dated at the end for the convenience of the reader who wishes to check it against the publication record of Lowry's books.

INTRODUCTION

George Woodcock

Writing a decade ago in *Canadian Literature*, the American critic, Robert B. Heilman, could still talk of the admirers of Malcolm Lowry's *Under the Volcano* as a "semi-secret order with a somewhat odd, quite small, but very dispersed membership." It was, also, an order with a limited field in which its admiration could be deployed, since *Under the Volcano* was then the only book by Lowry readily available. *Hear Us O Lord From Heaven Thy Dwelling Place* appeared in the same year as Heilman's article; Lowry's early and virtually unobtainable novel, *Ultramarine*, was not reissued until 1962. There followed through the sixties volumes of poems and letters, the novella *Lunar Caustic*, and the edited versions of the two incomplete novels, *Dark as the Grave Wherein My Friend Is Laid* and *October Ferry to Gabriola*.

This vast posthumous publication of the works of a writer who published little in his lifetime, is even now not complete. We are given to understand that there is a second volume of stories to come, and a fuller collection of the poems; there is also the last uncompleted novel, *La Mordida*. This means that, even now, the critic who has been unable to travel to Vancouver and consult the Lowry archive in the University of British Columbia is still discussing a writer with whose total work he is of necessity unfamiliar. The unfolding of Lowry's achievement to the public eye has already taken fourteen years since his death in 1957, and it may still be several years — perhaps even another decade — before everything he wrote of publishable quality is finally available. And even then, until scholarly editors produce *variorum* editions embracing all the false starts and abandoned passages of his later works, we shall not know the fulness of that verbal inventiveness which in the end seemed to choke with its excess Lowry's will to complete any book.

Because, roughly every other year since 1961, a hitherto unknown Lowry work (unknown at least to the public) has been published, the criticism of his writings has inevitably assumed a tentativeness that parallels Lowry's own massive hesitancies. His *aficionados* are no longer — and have not been since the mid-sixties — the "semi-secret order" of which Heilman wrote. The cult has come out of the catacombs, and Lowry has indeed been subjected to the kind of popularization, based mainly on the aura of romantic self-destructiveness that enwraps his life, which is not entirely appropriate to a writer so complex and in so deep but obscure a manner revelatory of the agonies of our age. But the critic has still been faced with the possibility that the next volume to be plucked from the air-conditioned shelves of the archive may somehow dislodge any verdict he has reached. And so a habit has arisen among writers on Lowry of making their discreet bows to the books yet unpublished, and of declaring themselves as unfinal in their judgement as the author himself.

This situation has had the healthy effect of postponing until Lowry's reputation has settled to some fairly stable level the writing of anything that might count as a major critical or biographical study. Only one book on Lowry has yet appeared and that — Perle Epstein's *The Private Labyrinth of Malcolm Lowry* — deals with merely one aspect (the Cabbalistic) of *Under the Volcano*. Two brief general studies in series that cater mainly for the campus market will shortly be published. Otherwise we are still at the stage where a multi-faceted collection of essays, dealing with Lowry's varied aspects and marking the shifts in critical attitude towards him, may be more useful than a premature attempt at definitive treatment.

This is the function the present volume is meant to fulfil. It intends to present the works, the man, and the sources in himself and his world from which he constructed what — again to quote Robert Heilman — can be described as "a multivalued poetic fiction, with its picture of the ailing soul, its sense of horrifying dissolution, and its submerged, uncertain vision of a hard new birth off in clouded time" which "is apparently the especial labour of the artistic conscience at our turn of the epoch."

From the beginning, as editor of *Canadian Literature*, a journal originating in a region peculiarly associated with Lowry, and published by the University that holds his papers, I felt it of peculiar importance and appropriateness to seek a range of critical articles that might eventually form a spectrum of observation and opinion illuminating Lowry's writings and their sources. Two special issues of *Canadian Literature* have been devoted to Lowry; individual writings by and on him have appeared in other issues; these form the basis of the present collection, but other essays, hitherto unpublished, have been added.

I have proceeded on the assumption that in the critical eye the works of a writer must always take precedence over the writer himself, and the collection therefore begins with a series of essays which consider all the works of fiction that Lowry regarded as important — *Under the Volcano, Hear Us O Lord From Heaven Thy Dwelling Place, Lunar Caustic, Dark as the Grave Wherein My Friend Is Laid* and *October Ferry to Gabriola*.

There is a sense — a visionary sense — in which Lowry, even when he wrote in prose, was entirely a poet; he himself compared the great trilogy he planned but never completed to Dante's work rather than Proust's. But at the same time as he wrote the ambitious poetic fictions on which his reputation will always principally rest, he also produced, copiously and often in many versions, a great many lyric poems of fine quality, and a selection of these, with notes by his friend and fellow-poet, Earle Birney, forms the bridge to the second, more biographical part of the collection.

Here Lowry — who has already spoken to us in the first part through the Preface to the French edition of *Under the Volcano* — appears again in his own voice in hitherto unpublished letters, and in the essays in which Hilda Thomas discusses his published letters and Downie Kirk tells of the Lowry he knew through correspondence. In a period when intermedia — the cross-fertilization of art by art — is a matter of especial interest, Lowry appropriately takes his place. His mental world was shaped not only by direct experience and books, which he read in prodigious variety, but also by his passions for jazz music and for the cinema. And I suggest that the essays published here on his reading and on his interests in music and film are among the most valuable in the collection because, by concentrating on special fields of preoccupation outside his writing (though of course by transmutation inside as well) they reveal a great deal in an intensive way about the nature of Lowry's creativity.

Indeed, it seems to me that, because of their intensiveness, they also reveal more about the man himself than the items which present direct personal recollections. I do not mean to belittle the essays which perform that function. William McConnell, a Vancouver lawyer who is also a short story writer and runs a private press, and Maurice Carey, a man of unliterary pretensions who was Lowry's host in his early days in Vancouver, present interesting partial views of Lowry. But one is aware how much the essential Lowry, that shy and defenceless man, has eluded them and so evades the reader. I have experienced the same sense of the essential absence of the whole man in talking to people who had known Lowry much more intimately — to his brother Stuart in England, for instance, and to his Cambridge friend, the late John Davenport. Each had his own Lowry to reveal, but neither of them was entirely the man who wrote *Under the Volcano* or *October Ferry to Gabriola*. Yet if we assume that the heroes of those books are in any more literal sense portraits of Lowry we are risking benightment in that maze of personal ambiguity to which every writer surrenders himself by the very act of creation. I suspect that Lowry will be the despair of his biographer.

THERE IS ONE BOOK by Lowry which has not received separate treatment in any essay of this book, though allusions to it recur. That is his first novel, *Ultramarine*. In his later years Lowry regarded the book with disfavour, and he did not allow it to be reprinted while he was alive. But, though greatly inferior to *Under the Volcano* in quality of writing and in breadth of conception, *Ultramarine* is not really a book one can regard as a discredit to a writer in his early twenties, and it is unfortunate that in general critics have followed Lowry's lead, and avoided this early work which in many interesting ways anticipates the later novels. It is a measure of the book's neglect that, while every year I am asked as editor to consider several essays on other works by Lowry, I have never received one on *Ultramarine*. It may not, therefore, be out of place for me to sketch out a view of this early novel in anticipation of the essays on the rest of Lowry's fiction with which this book begins.

In 1927, when he was not yet eighteen, Lowry sailed as a ship's boy on a cargo steamer bound for China and Japan. *Ultramarine* tells the story of a boy who set out on a similar enterprise. But the mere voyage is not the real theme of the novel, whose "dreamed-of-harbour" is rather the proving of one's self among other men.

It begins with the hero, Hilliot, already in the China Seas, recollecting the day he signed on for the ship "Nawab"; the day he chose, in his own mind, the men who would become his friends upon the voyage. His expectations have not been satisfied; the barrier of class — for he is an intellectual's son seeking experience — has risen between him and his shipmates, and his voyage has been a long effort to break out of his loneliness by winning the precious acceptance of the rest of the crew. His efforts to work well are treated with contempt; his intentions of proving himself sexually in the brothels of the Oriental seaports are frustrated by indecision and end in bouts of drunkenness which are self-righteously condemned by the rest of the crew. In the end a trivial incident resolves the situation and turns the cook, Andy, his great enemy, into a friend. A pigeon,

4

which one of the men has rescued from the topmast and has kept as a pet, falls into the harbour because its wings have been clipped; Hilliot tries to jump in and save it, but the other men restrain him because they think the waters are infested by sharks. The incident creates a comradeship, and the death of the captive that can neither fly nor swim releases Hilliot from the particular cage of his own loneliness. He does not soar far, it is true. He is accepted as a seaman, and yet at this final point his longing for the life he has left behind, and for the girl who represents it in his mind, is renewed. The past triumphs, and we know, as the novel ends, that what Hilliot has striven for, now it is gained, is wished no longer. The "dreamed-of-harbour" has changed its name and in his heart he is already on a different voyage. He is, like the hero of *October Ferry* so many years later, "outward bound".

Ultramarine is written consistently from Hilliot's inner point of view, in passages of interior monologue, largely reminiscent and ranging back into his childhood and away to Norway and England and to the girl Janet he has loved in both lands, alternating with passages of dialogue on the part of the crew which he sometimes overhears and sometimes shares in. It is largely derivative, but it anticipates the liberation into originality of Lowry's greater novel. The influence of Conrad Aiken's *Blue Voyage* was freely admitted by Lowry, while in the centre of the novel there is an elaborate rendering of a drunken night in an Eastern port which is reminiscent of Joyce's *Ulysses*, yet also looks forward to the great nightmare debauch in which *Under the Volcano* reaches its culmination and the hero, Geoffrey Firmin, dies by murder.

In *Ultramarine*, lived experience is incompletely fused into fiction; the general weakness of pattern and the particular weakness of characterization are accentuated by the nostalgic self-pity that pursues the hero from beginning to end. Yet much of the matter of his early novel finds its way, transformed, into *Under the Volcano*, and its experiments with time and memory, with the reality of the past making the present unreal, will be repeated in all the major novels. A reading of it is indispensable to a full understanding of Lowry.

I WOULD END in expressing my thanks, more directly than in mere acknowledgement, to Margerie Lowry for her cordial co-operation both in the preparation of the special issues of *Canadian Literature* devoted to Malcolm Lowry, and in granting the necessary permission to reprint the items by him contained in the present volume. (1971)

PART I

The Works

PREFACE TO A NOVEL

Malcolm Lowry

This preface to the French edition of *Under the Volcano*, which casts considerable light on Malcolm Lowry's view of his own novel, was prepared while Malcolm Lowry was working with Clarisse Françillon on her translation of his novel; the final version was actually prepared in French from Lowry's English notes, so that no English original exists. The following translation has been made by George Woodcock. The edition of *Under the Volcano* in which the preface appeared was published by Corréâ and the Club Français du Livre in 1949 and reprinted by Corréâ in 1960.

I LIKE PREFACES. I read them. Sometimes I do not read any farther, and it is possible that you may do the same. In that case, this preface will have failed in its purpose, which is to make your access to my book a little more easy. Above all, reader, do not regard these pages as an affront to your intelligence. They prove rather that the author here and there questions his own.

To begin with, his very style may assume an embarrassing resemblance to that of the German writer Schopenhauer describes, who wished to express six things at the same time instead of discussing them one after the other. "In those long, rich parenthetical periods, like boxes enclosing boxes, and crammed more full than roast geese stuffed with apples, one's memory above all is put to the task, when understanding and judgement should have been called upon to do their work."

But to take a criticism of style—as Schopenhauer conceived it—as a criticism of the mind and character of the author or even, as others would like, of the man himself, is beside the point. That at least is what I wrote in 1946, on board a bauxite ship in the middle of the waves between New Orleans and Port-au-Prince.

That preface was never published. As for this one, the first reason for my drafting it was the fact that in 1945 my book received a very lukewarm welcome from an English firm (which has since done me the honour of publishing it). Although the publishers considered the work "important and honest", they suggested wide corrections which I was reluctant to make. (You would have reacted in the same way had you written a book and been so tormented by it that you rejected and rewrote it many times.) Among other things, I was advised to suppress two or three characters, to reduce the twelve chapters to six, to change the subject, which was too similar to that of *Poison*; in short, to throw my book out of the window and write another. Since now I have the honour of being translated into French, I take up once again my letter of reply to my publisher and friend in London. The enterprise was doubtless a foolish one: to give all kinds of good esoteric reasons why the work should stay just as it was in the beginning.

Those reasons I have now almost completely forgotten, and perhaps that is lucky for you. It is in fact all too true, as Sherwood Anderson has remarked, that in all concerning his work a writer assumes the most extraordinary pretensions and is ready to justify anything. It is also likely that one of the few honest remarks an author has ever made was that of Julien Green on the subject, I believe, of his masterly *Minuit*: "My intention was—and has ever since remained to me—obscure."

In writing this book, which was started when I was twenty-six (I am now about to salute my fortieth year) and finished five years ago, my intention did not at first seem to me obscure, although it became more so as the years went on. But, whether obscure or not, it still remains a fact that one of my intentions was to write a book.

And, indeed, my intention was not to write a tedious book. I do not believe a single author, even the most irascible of them all, has ever had the deliberate intention of wearying his reader, though it has been said that boredom can be used as a technique. But once this book did in fact appear boring to a reader — and a professional reader at that — I thought it necessary to reply to the observations of that professional reader, and here is the gist of what I wrote. All this may perhaps appear to you terribly vain and pompous, but how can you explain to someone who claims to have been bored by your prose that he was in the wrong for letting himself be bored?

"Dear Sir," I wrote then, "Thank you for your letter of the 29th November, 1945. I received it only on New Year's Eve. Moreover, it reached me here in Mexico where, entirely by chance, I am living in the tower which served as a model for the house of one of my characters. Ten years ago I had only seen that tower from the outside, and — in chapter VI — it became the place where my hero too experienced some slight vexations as a result of delayed mail. . . ."

Then I went on to say that if my work had already assumed the classic form of the printed page instead of the sad and desolate aspect which characterizes an unpublished manuscript, the opinion of the reader would certainly have been entirely different because of the various critical judgements that would have assailed his ears. Since the tiresomeness or otherwise of the beginning of *Under the Volcano* appeared to me dependent on the reader's state of mind, on his readiness to seize the author's intention, I suggested — doubtless in desperation of my cause — that a brief preface might neutralize the reactions which my professional reader foresaw. I continued thus: "If you tell me that a good wine needs no label, I may perhaps reply that I am not talking about wine but about mescal, and that even more than a label — once one has crossed the threshold of the tavern — mescal calls for the accompaniment of both salt and lemon. I hope at least that such a preface may bring a little lemon and salt."

In this way I wrote a letter of round about 20,000 words, which took me the time I might just as well have employed on starting the first draft of a new novel, even more boring than the other. And since, in the eyes of my reader, the first chapter seemed to be the novel's greatest crime, I limited myself to an analysis of that long first chapter which establishes the themes and counter-themes of the book, which sets the tone, which harmonizes the symbolism.

The narrative, I explained, begins on All Souls' Day, in November, 1939, in a hotel called Casino de la Selva — selva meaning *wood*. And perhaps it would not be out of place to mention here that the book was first of all conceived rather pretentiously on the sempiternal model of Gogol's *Dead Souls*, and as the first leaf of the triptych of a kind of drunken *Divine Comedy*. *Purgatory* and *Paradise* were to follow, with the protagonist, like Chichikov, becoming at each stage slightly better or worse, according to one's point of view. (However, if one is to believe a recent authority, the incredible Vladimir Nabokov, the progression postulated by Gogol was rather: Crime, Punishment, Redemption; Gogol threw almost all of Punishment and Redemption into the fire.) The theme of the dark wood, introduced once again in chapter VII when the Consul enters a lugubrious cantina called El Bosque, which also means *wood*, is resolved in chapter IX, which relates the death of the heroine and in which the wood becomes reality and also fatality.

This first chapter is shown through the eyes of a French film producer, Jacques

Laruelle. He establishes a kind of survey of the terrain, just as he expresses the slow, melancholy and tragic rhythm of Mexico itself: Mexico, the meeting place of many races, the ancient battleground of social and political conflicts where, as Waldo Frank, I believe, has shown, a colourful and talented people maintained a religion which was virtually a cult of death. It is the ideal setting for the struggle of a human being against the powers of darkness and light.

After leaving the Casino de la Selva, Jacques Laruelle finds himself looking into the barranca which plays a great part in the story, and which is also the ravine, that cursed abyss which in our age every man presents to himself, and also, more simply, if the reader prefers it, the sewer.

The chapter ends in another cantina where people are taking refuge during an unseasonal storm, while elsewhere, all over the world, people are crawling into the air-raid shelters; then the lights go out, just as, all over the world as well, they are going out. Outside, in that night created by the tempest, the luminous wheel is turning.

That wheel is the Ferris wheel erected in the middle of the square, but it is also, if you like, many other things: the wheel of the law, the wheel of Buddha. It is even eternity, the symbol of the Everlasting Return. That wheel, which demonstrates the very form of the book, can also be considered in a cinematographic manner as the wheel of Time, which is about to turn in an inverse direction, until we reach the preceding year. For the beginning of the second chapter brings us to All Souls' Day a year before, in November, 1938.

AT THIS POINT I tried modestly to insinuate that my little book seemed to me denser and deeper, composed and carried out with more care than the English publisher supposed; that if its meanings had escaped the reader, or if the latter had deemed uninteresting the meanings that float on the surface of the narrative, this might have been due at least in part to a merit rather than a failing of mine. In fact, had not the more accessible aspect of the book been designed so carefully that the reader did not wish to take the trouble of pausing to go below the surface? "If that is true," I added, not without a certain vanity, "for how many books can it be said?"

In a more sentimental tone, but with only an appearance of greater modesty, I then wrote as follows: "Since I am asking for a re-reading of the *Volcano*, in the light of certain aspects which may not have occurred to you, and since I do not wish to undertake a defence of every paragraph, it may be as well for me to admit that in my view the principal failing of the book, from which all the others flow, lies in something which cannot be remedied: the mental baggage of the book is subjective rather than objective; it would better suit a poet — I do not say a good poet — than a novelist, and it is a baggage very difficult to carry as far as its destination. On the other hand, just as a tailor who knows his customer's deformity tries to hide it, I have tried as far as possible to hide the faults of my understanding. But since the conception of the work was primarily poetic, these deformities may hardly matter after all. Besides, poems often call for several readings before their meaning is revealed — is exposed in the mind as I believe Hopkins said — and it is precisely that notion which you have overlooked."

I demanded the most serious examination of the text, and I asked how, without appreciating its contents, the reader had reached his view that the book was too long, particularly since his reaction might well be different after a second reading. Did not readers, just as much as authors, take a risk of falling over themselves by going too fast? And what a boring book it must be if so hasty a reading were all that could be granted!

I went on to explain that my novel consists of twelve chapters, and the main part of the narrative is contained within a single day of twelve hours. In the same way, there are twelve months in a year and the whole book is enclosed within the limits of a year, while that deeper layer of the novel — or the poem — which derives from myth is linked at this point with the Jewish Cabbala, where the number twelve is of the greatest importance. The Cabbala is used for poetic ends because it represents Man's spiritual aspirations. The Tree of Life, its emblem, is a kind of complicated ladder whose summit is called Kether, or Light, while somewhere in its midst an abyss opens out. The spiritual domain of the Consul is probably Qliphoth, the world of husks and demons, represented by the Tree of Life turned upside down and governed by Beelzebub, the God of Flies. All this was not essential for the understanding of the book; I mentioned it in passing so as to give the feeling, as Henry James has said, "that depths exist."

In the Jewish Cabbala the abuse of magic powers is compared to drunkenness or the abuse of wine, and is expressed, if I remember rightly, by the Hebrew word *sod*. Another attribution of the word *sod* signifies garden, or neglected garden, and the Cabbala itself is sometimes considered a garden (naturally similar to that where grew the tree of forbidden fruit which gave us the Knowledge of Good and Evil), with the Tree of Life planted in the middle. In one way or another these matters are at the base of many of our legends regarding the origins of man, and William James, if not Freud, might be in agreement with me when I affirm that the agonies of the drunkard find a very close parallel in the agonies of the mystic who has abused his powers. Here the Consul has brought everything together in a magnificently drunken fashion. In Mexico, mescal is a formidable drink but a drink which one can get in any cantina much more easily, if I may say so, than Scotch whisky in the Impasse des Deux-Anges. (Let me say in passing that I see I have done wrong to mescal and tequila, which are drinks I like very much, and for that I should perhaps present my apologies to the Mexican government.) But mescal is also a drug which is taken in the form of mescalin, and the transcendance of its effects is one of the best-known experiments among occultists. It seems as though the Consul has confused the two states, and perhaps after all he is not in the wrong.

This novel, to use a phrase of Edmund Wilson, has for its subject the forces that dwell within man and lead him to look upon himself with terror. Its subject is also the fall of man, his remorse, his incessant struggle towards the light under the weight of the past, which is his destiny. The allegory is that of the Garden of Eden, the garden representing the world from which we are now even a little more under the threat of ejection than at the moment when I wrote this book. On one level, the drunkenness of the Consul may be regarded as symbolising the universal drunkenness of war, of the period that precedes war, no matter when. Throughout the twelve chapters, the destiny of my hero can be considered in its relationship to the destiny of humanity.

"I hold to the number twelve," I then added. "It is as if I heard a clock sounding midnight for Faust, and when I think of the slow progression of the chapters, I feel that neither more nor less than twelve should satisfy me. For the rest, the book is stratified in numerous planes. My effort has been to clarify as far as possible whatever at first presented itself to me in a complicated and esoteric manner. The novel can be read simply as a novel during which you may — if you wish — skip whole passages, but from which you will get far more if you skip nothing at all. It can be regarded as a kind of symphony or opera, or even as something like a cowboy film. I wanted to make of it a jam session, a poem, a song, a tragedy, a comedy, a farce. It is superficial, profound, entertaining, boring, according to one's taste. It is a prophecy, a political warning, a cryptogram, a crazy film, an absurdity, a writing on the wall. It can be thought of as a kind of machine; it works, you may be sure, for I have discovered that to my own expense. And in case you should think that I have made of it everything except a novel, I shall answer that in the last resort it is a real novel that I have intended to write, and even a damnably serious novel."

In short, I made terrific efforts to explain my own idea of this unfortunate volume; I waged a notable battle for the work as it stood, as it was finally printed, and as it today appears for my French readers. And remember, I wrote all that in Mexico, in the very place where ten years before I had started my book, and in the end I received, from the hands of the same tiny postman who brought the Consul his delayed postcard, the news that it had been accepted.

After this long preamble, my dear French reader, it would perhaps be honest of me to admit to you that the idea I cherished in my heart was to create a pioneer work in its own class, and to write at last an authentic drunkard's story. I do not know whether I have succeeded. And now, friend, I beg you continue your walk along the Seine, and please replace this book where you found it, in the second-hand bookseller's 100-franc box.

MALCOLM LOWRY,
September, 1948.

THE POSSESSED ARTIST
AND THE AILING SOUL

Robert B. Heilman

To HAVE BEEN AN ORIGINAL ADMIRER of Malcolm Lowry's
Under the Volcano, and to remain an admirer for almost a decade and a half,
is very much like belonging to a semi-secret order with a somewhat odd, quite
small, but widely dispersed membership. It is a very loose order, without adopted
procedure and certainly without programme. Membership is conferred by taste, not
sought by will or exercised through evangelical rigour. Members become known
to each other only when they discover each other by accident. The big point is
that such discoveries do continue to be made, year after year, in more than one
part of the English-reading world. Yet they are an insistent trickle rather than a
growing stream that could be converted into a literary power system. Whoever
has read Lowry has been unforgettably impressed, but readers have been, it
appears, strangely few. The slender society of those who esteem him, whatever
the strength of their convictions, have been given to contemplation rather than to
promotion or even public debate: he remains a private possession rather than a
public figure — far less established in a literary niche than, say, either Nathanael
West or Djuna Barnes, whom in some way he brings to mind and who hardly
have a greater claim upon our respect. Perhaps the disinclination of Lowry
admirers to shout from the housetops is related to a certain meticulousness in
their literary judgement: they customarily speak of *Under the Volcano* as a distinguished "minor" work or as a "minor classic". This reserve is understandable;
despite the often kaleidoscopic movement of both outer and inner landscape,
there is some limitedness of scope, some incompleteness of human range, some
circumscribing of consciousness that is felt partly in the fewness of the dramatis
personae and partly in the enclosing illness of the protagonist (though in saying
this last, one must always be mindful that the ailing soul may have extraordinary
visions). But the use of "minor" is not an inadvertent disparagement: it is an

16

honourable by-product of that need to place which is felt only when the novel in question arouses the conviction that it is not an entertainment of the year but a work of art that will be valid for many other years.

If a historian leafed through the journals of 1947 and noted the new novels reviewed, he would not find another one written in English, I surmise, that has achieved a more durable quiet esteem than *Under the Volcano* (I exclude Mann's *Doctor Faustus*, to which I shall return later). It has survived in a "population" where the normal death rate is close to 100%. A minor irony: in America it has survived its own publishing house. It has survived, as we have noted, an apparent smallness of canvas, and it has also survived a quite opposite difficulty: a fecundity of suggestive detail that tends to over-stimulate the imagination, that is, to set it off in more ways than can be decently encompassed within an overall design. Something survives beyond the sense of chaos that the fecundity is in danger of creating, beyond an impression of a tropical creative richness (this in itself, of course, is not to be disparaged, even when it is imperfectly controlled). What survives, again, is something beyond the quality usually called "intensity", though the stresses that Lowry images, luxuriantly and often fantastically, do induce the severe tautness that marks some kinds of aesthetic experience. Intensity is really a secondary virtue; it can be attached to superficial forms of action (of the order of fisticuffs, for instance), just as more profound experience can be transmitted in relatively un-taut moods such as the contemplative. The criterion is not the presence of intensity but the depth of the concern — the spiritual burden — that intensity accompanies. The less substantial the matter, the more the hard and gemlike flame will resemble ordinary flushed cheeks and fever that can be aspirined away. The fire in *Under the Volcano* is not easily put out.

The sense of a largeness that somehow bursts out of the evident constriction, the fertility that borders on the excessive and the frenzied, the intensity that is not a surrogate for magnanimity, and finally an apprehension of reality so vivid that it seems to slide over into madness — these are symptoms of the work of the "possessed" artist. If he has not quite achieved majority, Lowry belongs to the possessed novelists, among whom the great figures are Dostoevsky and Melville and, some of the time, Dickens. They may be distinguished from the "self-possessed" artists: Thackeray and Trollope and, to snatch an example from current fashion, C. P. Snow. Or, since Lowry's theme is human disaster, a grievous, driving, frenetic disaster, let us take for contrast Hardy, who seems calmly to organize and impose disaster as if he were seated at some cosmic control panel. In an older writer like Hawthorne or a modern one like R. P. Warren, there is somewhat of a conflict, or even an alternation, of possession and self-possession, of an unbridled urgency and a controlling will. The possessed artist is in the tradition of Plato's Ion, and at the risk of too neat a polarity, it may be hazarded that the self-possessed artist has ties with Aristotle's Poetics: rational analysability of form appears to imply rational creatability of form. It is not altogether a parody to picture the self-possessed artist, deep browed at his drawing board, coolly planning plot and catharsis. In C. P. Snow the key line, a recurrent one, is surely, "May I have a word with you, Lewis?" "A word" — a council — a plan — logos and logistics: life is ordered, or, if it does not wholly accede to the order designed for it, what dissidence there is is reflected, not in unruly surges of action that in their way elude the author and his decorous creatures, but through the rational comment of observers. Things never get out of hand; no wild dogs tug at the trainer's leash. Perhaps the ultimate figure in the world of self-possession is Arnold Bennett: one of his major aims seems to have been to keep his characters down, to remain the unyielding bailiff on his huge Five Towns estate. Was not this — that he would never "let go" — a subtle ingredient in what Virginia Woolf had against him? That, really, he saw Mrs. Brown only in terms of attributes that were at his beck and call? Bennett illustrates the intimate relationship, the virtual identity, between self-possession and the rigorous domination of character and scene (or at least the air of this). In some way his sense of security seems to have been involved in his paternal tyranny: for his creatures, no out of bounds, no fractiousness, no unpredicted courses, no iddish cutting loose. And if V. S. Pritchett is right, Bennett suffered accordingly: his self-possession was close to suicidal.

Such comparisons help us to place Lowry. In sum: the self-possessed artist — the one who uses his materials as an instrument. The possessed artist — the materials appear to use him as an instrument, finding in him, as it were, a channel to the objective existence of art, sacrificing a minimum of their autonomy to his hand, which partly directs and shapes rather than wholly controls. This is how it is with Lowry. If *Under the Volcano* is a more talented book than any one of the outstanding C. P. Snow novels and is still less well known, it is in part that the work of the self-possessed artist is more accessible, less threatening, farther away from anguish; even in Hardy the inimical and the destructive are in an odd way almost sterilized because for the most part they originate in an outer world that is unyielding or uncontrollable only by fits and starts, rather than in an inner realm of constants where catastrophe is always latent (Sue Bridehead is a rare exception). Snow works in a wider and more accommodating territory, Lowry in a very much more dangerous terrain. Possessed work may open up any depth before one, any abyss in other personalities or in one's own. It does not primarily contemplate, though it does not ignore, the ailing world, which is generally reparable in Snow, or traditionally irreparable in naturalist fiction. Rather its theme is the ailing soul. It is an ancient theme whose history concerns us here only in that in our day the theme is used with extraordinary frequency. Whether it is that illness is especially attractive to us because we find in it a novel window to reality, or an apparently better window to reality, than the less clinical ones that we have principally relied on; or that the culture is sick, as some critics aver with almost tedious constancy, and that as a consequence we must, to avoid self-deception and serve truth, contemplate only sickness — these differing conclusions are arguable.

In the contemporary use of illness, at any rate, we find quite different perspectives. In *Sound and Fury* there are various ailing souls: through them we have a complex view of decadence and of a contrasting vitality. In Robbe-Grillet's *Voyeur* clinical disorder of personality is itself the aesthetic object: despite all that has been said about Robbe-Grillet's innovations in the vision of reality, the final effect is one of a disturbingly ingenious tour de force. In *Magic Mountain* the ailment of the soul is intricately intertwined with that of the body; a host of theoretical salvations are examined, and the final note is one of hope through a surprisingly simple practical therapy. But in *Doctor Faustus* there is a more fundamental and violent illness of soul, a counterpart of a more fundamental and violent illness of body, one that is in effect chosen; we see a sick person and a sick era, sick thought that is a culmination of a tradition; yet a tradition in which the paradoxical affiliation of the destructive and the creative is terrifying.

Doctor Faustus offers some instructive parallels with *Under the Volcano*: both works belong to 1947; both recount the spiritual illness of a man that is in some way akin to the illness of an age; both glance at the politics of the troubled 1930's, but both are artistically mature enough to resist the temptations always offered by the political theme — the polemic tone, the shrill "J'accuse." Instead they contemplate the failures of spirit of which the political disorders are a symptom. They do this differently. Though both draw on the Faustian theme, Lowry introduces it less directly than suggestively, as one strand in a mythic fabric of considerable richness. Mann, by now an old hand at mythic reconstructions, revives Faustus in the grand manner. The mode of evil is affirmative: demonic possession, a rush into destruction in a wild flare of self-consuming, power-seizing creativity. In demonic possession there is a hypertrophy of ego; Lowry's hero, on the contrary, suffers from a kind of undergrowth of soul. One leaps on life rapaciously; the other falls short of the quality that makes life possible. Both the rape and the agonizing insufficiency are done with hair-raising immediacy. But Mann's style is heroic, whereas Lowry's stage is domestic. Geoffrey Firmin (the infirm Geoffrey) is more of a private figure than Adrian Leverkühn ; his life has less amplitude in itself; in the concrete elements of it there is not the constant pressure toward epical-allegorical aggrandizement. But this is a statement of a difference, not of a deficiency. Both novelists are possessed; both seem to be the instruments of a vision whose autarchy they do not impair as they assist its emergence into public form. This is true of Mann, despite his usual heavy component of expository pages; it is true of Lowry, despite some artifice and frigidity in the narrative arrangements.

If Lowry's work is, compared with Mann's, "domestic", nevertheless the implied analogy with domestic tragedy is slight at best. To make one important contrast: Lowry has a range of tone that household drama never had. In fact, even in the orbit of possessed artists, his range is unusual: in recording a disaster of personality that is on the very edge of the tragic, he has an extravagant comic sense that creates an almost unique tension among moods. Desperation, the ludicrous, nightmare, the vulgar, the appalling, the fantastic, the nonsensical, and the painfully pathetic coexist in an incongruous melange that is still a unity. The serious historian of the ailing soul may achieve the bizarre, but he rarely works through humour or finds the Lowry fusion of the ridiculous and the ghastly. With Lowry, the grotesque seems always about to trip up the catastrophic, the silly to spike the portentous, the idiotic to collapse the mad. When evil is present, it is more likely to be nasty than sinister. The assailing demons tend to be mean little gremlins; in a way, Geoffrey's disaster is the triumph of meanness, not as a case-history of an eccentric flop, but as a universal image of man in the smallness to which he is always liable. This can take on its own dreadfulness, partly because petty vice contains echoes of major failures, partly because nemesis is not trivial, and partly because there is always maintained a touching nostalgia for a large and noble selfhood. In *Lady Windermere's Fan* there is a very bad line about man's being in the gutter but looking at the stars; it is bad because the play contains no vestige of real gutters or real stars, so that words alone are being exploited. But these antithetical images could be used of *Under the Volcano* without bathos, for it contains some of the more plausible gutters in modern fiction while portraying the survival, even in them, of a dim and struggling consciousness of other worlds. Lowry is quite lucid about what is sickness and what is health, rather more so, indeed, than another possessed novelist usually credited with expertise in these polar states, D. H. Lawrence.

Lowry does not manage the cosmic texture of events that we find in *Doctor Faustus*, but there is an extraordinary texture of symbol and allusion. It is doubtless natural for the possessed novelist to call on many of the resources of poetry. The self-possessed novelist is not necessarily prosaic or shallow or one-dimensional, witness Henry James; but in the main we image him as forging steadily or deliberately ahead, on the direct prose route to his end. The possessed writer has an air of battling, not quite successfully, with a multitude of urgencies that come at him from all sides and fling off again on their own, not always forced into a common direction. If the overt action of *Under the Volcano* is slight, the metaphorical action is intense. Numerous objects, properties, occurrences, and even ideas, recollections, and observations not only exist in their own right but also work figuratively or symbolically. The nexuses are imaginative rather than casual, or logical, or chronological; hiatuses compel a high attention; dextrous leaps are called for. In such a sense the novel is "poetic", not in the sense that a mistily atavistic syntax and a solemn iambic hauteur, as often in the self-conscious experimental theatre, pass for poetic.

The "story", as I have said, is slight: Yvonne, the wife of alcoholic Geoffrey Firmin, returns, after a year's separation, to her husband in Mexico. The events all take place on the day of her return. Geoffrey's passing desires to pull out with Yvonne are overcome by a far more urgent passion for alcohol. A French movie-producer, former lover of Yvonne, is with them for a while and incredulously lectures Geoffrey. Geoffrey's brother Hugh, ex-reporter and sailor, now about to run arms to the Spanish loyalists, in love with Yvonne, spends the day with them. The chief event is an outing by bus — Lowry's own wayward bus ("making its erratic journey"), which stops for a while near a wounded Indian left by the roadside but leaves without anybody's having done anything. Late in the day Geoffrey, who has constantly been getting separated from Hugh and Yvonne, outrageously abuses Yvonne and runs into the woods near Popocatepetl. Yvonne and Hugh pursue. Yvonne and Geoffrey lose their lives by means symbolically associated with the episode of the unattended roadside Indian.

Hugh makes his boat for Spain: this we have learned from a retrospective prologue — the contents of which are certain words and thoughts of the French movie-man a year after the day of the main story. This prologue is supposed to introduce all the main themes; but there is too much there to assimilate, especially since most of the material is not dramatized. It is a cold beginning, and then one has to keep going back to it as to a table of contents — which is not the kind of re-reading that a concentrated book may legitimately demand. Further, on technical matters: the retrospects on which a one-day story must rely tend to be flaccid in style (Hugh's) or foggy in detail (Yvonne's); and coincidence has a fairly large hand in things. But, once into the story, one is less aware of these things than of the imaginative richness. The minds of the characters are sensitive recording instruments, tenacious alike of facts and of their suggestive value. The book is a cornucopia of images; both the psychic and the outer world have a tangibility which a thoughtless slice of realism could never produce; humour and horror are never alleged but are moulded into a hard and yet resilient narrative substance. Always one is driven to follow through on the evocations that trail off behind the foreground facts.

So, besides reading the story as story, we are always aware of a multitude of implications which, in their continual impingement upon us, remind us of the recurrent images of Shakespeare. The action takes place in November, on the Day of the Dead; Geoffrey feels his "soul dying"; a funeral takes place; burial customs, the shipping of a corpse are discussed; an earlier child of Yvonne's is dead; Geoffrey thinks he is seeing a dead man; a cantina is called La Sepultura; Geoffrey recalls Dr. Faustus's death; a dead dog is seen in a ravine; a dying Indian is found by the roadside. Always there are vultures, pariah dogs, the noise of target practice. There are a decaying hotel, a reference to the House of Usher, the ruins of the palace of Maximilian and Carlotta. Geoffrey's soul appears to him "a town ravaged and stricken"; an imaginary "little town by the sea" burns up. Frustrations and failures are everywhere — engagements are missed, the light fails in a cinema. Always we are reminded of the barranca or ravine, near the town — a fearful abyss. Once it is called "Malebolge"; there are various allusions to Dante's *Inferno*; Geoffrey feels he is in hell, quotes Dante on sin, looks at Cocteau's *La Machine Infernale*, takes a ride in a Maquina Infernal, calls ironically-defiantly, "I love hell"; at the end he is in a bar "under the volcano". "It was not for nothing the ancients had placed Tartarus under Mt. Aetna . . . ." There are continual references to Marlowe's Faustus, who could not pray for grace, just as Geoffrey cannot feel a love that might break his love for alcohol, or rather, symbolize a saving attitude; as in the Faustus play, *soul* is a recurrent word. There is an Eden-Paradise theme: a public sign becomes a motif in itself, being repeated at the end of the story: "Do you enjoy this garden, which is yours? Keep your children from destroying it!" Geoffrey once mistranslates the second sentence: "We evict those who destroy." Geoffrey's own garden, once beautiful, has become a jungle; he hides bottles in the shrubbery; and once he sees a snake there.

The lavish use of such rich resources reveals the possessed artist. They might serve, perhaps, only to create a vivid sequence of impressions, feelings, and moods. But Lowry is possessed by more than sensations and multiple associations; there is a swirl of passionate thoughts and ideas as well as passions; thought and feeling are fused, and always impressions and moods seem the threshold to meanings that must be entered. It seems to me that he seizes instinctively upon materials that have both sensory and suprasensory values. How present the central conception — that of the ailing soul? There are endless symbols for ill-being, from having cancer to taking dope. But Geoffrey's tremendous drinking is exactly the right one, or by art is made to seem the right one. In greater or lesser extent it is widely shared, or at least is related to widely practised habits; it is known to be a pathological state; it may be fatal, but also it can be cured. It lacks the ultimate sinisterness of dope, the irresistibility of cancer; hence it is more flexible, more translatable. And Lowry slowly makes us feel, behind the brilliantly presented facts of the alcoholic life, a set of meanings that make the events profoundly revelatory: drinking as an escape, an evasion of responsibility, a separation from life, a self-worship, a denial of love, a hatred of the living with a faith. (There is an always pressing guilt theme: Geoffrey, who was a naval officer in World War I, is a kind of sinning Ancient Mariner, caught by Life-in-Death, loathing his slimy creatures, born of the d.t.'s, whom he cannot expiatorily bless but must keep trying to drink away). The horror of Geoffrey's existence is always in the forefront of our consciousness, as it should be; but in the horror is involved an awareness of the dissolution of the old order, of the "drunken madly revolving world," of which Hugh says, "Good god, if our civilization were to sober up for a couple of days, it'd die of remorse on the third." At the end Geoffrey, unable by act of will to seize upon the disinterested aid of two old Mexicans, is the victim of local fascists: fascism preys upon a world that has already tossed away from its own soul.

The episode which most successfully unifies the different levels of meaning is that of the Indian left wounded by the roadside. He is robbed by a Spanish "pelado", a symbol of "the exploitation of everybody by everybody else." Here we have echoes of the Spanish Conquest and a symbol of aggression generally. Yvonne can't stand the sight of blood: it is her flaw, her way of acquiescing in the *de facto*. Geoffrey finds rules against doing anything; everyone feels that "it wasn't one's own business, but someone else's." It is modern irresponsibility and selfishness; the reader is prepared also to think of the "non-intervention" policy by the refrain which echoes throughout the book, "they are losing on the Ebro." But above all this is the story of the Good Samaritan — only there is no Samaritan. Devil take the least of these. (Geoffrey's ship, a gunboat disguised as a merchantman, has been named the *Samaritan* — a comment upon modern Samaritanism.)

Hugh, held back by Geoffrey, is almost the Good Samaritan — Hugh who is going to run arms to Spain. To Geoffrey and Yvonne, he is "romantic"; doubtless he is, and he has his own kind of guilt; but at least he insists on action, disinterested action. Here we come to what is apparently the basic theme of the book: man, in the words of a proverb repeated chorally, cannot live without love. Lowry flirts with the danger of the topical: the Spanish war might give the novel the air of a political tract. But ultimately, I think, the author does succeed in keeping the political phenomena on the periphery of the spiritual substance, using them for dramatic amplification of his metaphysic. It would be possible to read Geoffrey, always impersonally called the Consul, as dying capitalism, as laissez faire, or as sterile learning, like the speaker in Tennyson's *Palace of Art*. But such readings, though they are partly true, too narrowly circumscribe the total human situation with which Lowry is concerned.

THE CONSUL'S CLIMACTIC ACTS of hate are a world's confession. Yvonne thinks of the need "of finding some faith," perhaps in "unselfish love." Whence love is to be derived, or how sanctioned and disciplined, is a question which the symbols do not fully answer. Yet it is the effect of Lowry's allusions — Dante, Faustus — to push the imagination toward a final reality that transcends all historical presents, however much each present may comment upon and even modify it. Most of all this effect is secured by his constant allusion to Christian myth and history — the crucifixion, Golgotha, the last supper, original sin. Lowry is hardly writing a Christian allegory; indeed, some of the Christian echoes are decidedly ironic. But his whole complex of image and symbol is such as to direct a dissolving order, in search of a creative affirmation, toward that union of the personal and the universal which is the religious.

The two extremes which are the technical dangers of this kind of work are the tightly bound allegory, in which a system of abstract equivalents for all the concrete materials of the story constricts the imaginative experience, and a loose impressionism, in which a mass of suggestive enterprises sets off so many associations, echoes, and conjectures that the imaginative experience becomes crowded and finally diffuse. It is the latter risk that Lowry runs. For the present account, to avoid excessive length, consistently oversimplifies the ingredients that it deals with, and it fails to deal with many other ingredients — for instance, the guitar motif, the cockfight motif, the theme of mystics and mysteries, the recurrent use of Indians, horses, the movie *The Hands of Orlac*, etc. Lowry has an immensely rich and vigorous imagination, and he never corks his cornucopia of evocative images and symbols. Some disciplinary rejections, some diffidence in setting afloat upon the imagination every boat that he finds upon a crowded shore, would have reduced the distractedness to which the author is occasionally liable and would have concentrated and shaped the author's effect more clearly. This is to say, perhaps, that the possessed artist might at times borrow a little from the soul of the self-possessed artist. But if one might wish for a more ordered synthesis of parts, one would never want a diminution of the power of Lowry's possessed art. There is great life in what he has written — in his solid world of inner and outer objects in which the characters are dismayed and imprisoned as in Kafka's tales; and in the implicit coalescence of many levels of meaning that we find in Hermann Broch. Such a multivalued poetic fiction, with its picture of the ailing soul, its sense of horrifying dissolution, and its submerged, uncertain vision of a hard new birth off in clouded time, is apparently the especial labour of the artistic conscience at our turn of an epoch.

(1961)

FAUST AND
UNDER THE VOLCANO

Anthony R. Kilgallin

THE BEST INTRODUCTION to any critical study of *Under the Volcano* is Lowry's "Preface to a Novel", as presented in *Canadian Literature* 9, in which he analyzes "...that long first chapter which establishes the themes and counter-themes of the book, which sets the tone, which harmonizes the symbolism." The uppermost of these themes is that of Faust: "It is as if I heard a clock sounding midnight for Faust," writes Lowry in justifying his use of twelve chapters. The Consul Geoffrey Firmin, God-free and infirm, is a man fallen from Grace, in the Christian or Catholic sense, and a black magician on another plane. The entire novel is built upon the ramifications of his fall:

> This novel, to use a phrase of Edmund Wilson, has for its subject the forces that dwell within man and lead him to look upon himself with terror. Its subject is also the fall of man, his remorse, his incessant struggle towards the light under the weight of the past, which is his destiny ... Throughout the twelve chapters, the destiny of my hero can be considered in its relationship to the destiny of humanity.

The third epigraph to the novel is a quotation from Gothe's *Faust*: "Whosoever increasingly strives upward ... him can we save." Goethe himself set these lines in inverted commas in his masterpiece to emphasize them as a fundamental pronouncement. In his eighty-second year he spoke vital words to Eckermann about this passage:

> In these lines the key to Faust's salvation is contained: in Faust himself there is an activity mounting ever higher and purer to the end, and from above eternal love which helps him in his need. All this is completely in harmony with our religious conceptions, according to which we enter into bliss not by our own strength alone, but by the divine grace vouchsafed to us.

In terms of the Consul these lines are to be profoundly ironic.

The narrative of *Under the Volcano* opens on a "gigantic red evening, whose reflection bled away in the deserted swimming pools scattered everywhere like so many mirages." The metaphor is reminiscent of the famous line of Marlowe's Faustus: "See, see, where Christ's blood streams in the firmament!" as Faustus pleads for one drop of blood to save his soul. Geoffrey is first identified with Faustus through a related simile:

> What had happened just a year ago today seemed already to belong in a different age. One would have thought the horrors of the present would have swallowed it up like a drop of water. It was not so. Though tragedy was in the process of becoming unreal and meaningless, it seemed one was still permitted to remember the days when an individual life held some value and was not a mere misprint in a communiqué.

Almost the last of Faustus' pleas was, "O soul, be changed into little waterdrops,/ And fall into the ocean, ne'er be found!" In vain does Faustus seek an escape through anonymity. His tragedy, in fact, still serves as the best known archetype of its kind; likewise, the tragedy of the Consul's death is unforgettable.

Chapter one of the novel is presented through the consciousness of Jacques Laruelle, acquaintance since childhood of Geoffrey, and sometime movie-producer who has been considering "making in France a modern film version of the Faustus story with some such character as Trotsky for its protagonist." Unrecognized by Laruelle, Geoffrey's life has been this very story; it is purposefully ironic that ten months later Trotsky is murdered in Mexico City, an exile with a short pointed beard like the Consul who, on the night of his death, is to be called "Trotsky". To prepare for his movie, Laruelle has borrowed a volume of Elizabethan plays from Geoffrey himself, among which is Marlowe's *Doctor Faustus*. Opening the book at random he reads, "then will I headlong fly into the earth: / Earth, gape! it will not harbour me." He sits "oblivious of his surroundings, gazing at the words that seemed to have the power of carrying his own mind downward into a gulf, as in fulfilment on his own spirit of the threat Marlowe's Faustus had cast at his despair." Looking closer at the passage, he realizes he has misread the word "fly" for the actual word "run". This simple slip is intensified when, several pages later, we hear the line, "where I come from they don't run." The speaker is Weber, a witness to Geoffrey's murder, which, in Geoffrey's own way, was a literally physical attempt to enact Marlowe's quotation on his last night of life. The word "fly" calls to mind the inscription on Faustus' arm, "*Homo fuge*: whither should I fly."

Playing the game of "sortes Shakespeareanae" Laruelle turns again coincidentally to a quotation from *Doctor Faustus*:

> Cut is the branch that might have grown full straight,
> And burned is Apollo's laurel bough,
> That sometimes grew within this learned man,
> Faustus is gone; regard his hellish fall —

Geoffrey had "gone" exactly one year ago; the play's next line, "Whose fiendful fortune may exhort the wise," is a potential warning to Laruelle and to the reader to observe, and profit from, the example of Geoffrey the damned soul who supposedly had once considered writing an occult volume to be entitled "Secret Knowledge".

Inside the book of plays Laruelle finds an unsent letter of Geoffrey to Yvonne, his divorced wife, imploring her to return to him "if only for a day". That the Consul could not bring himself to send the letter, a plea for salvation, indicates partially his inability to communicate this desire. He writes, "But this is what it is to live in hell. I could not, cannot ask you. I could not, cannot send a telegram." Despite the Good Angel, Faustus is also unable to communicate his desire for deliverance. To confirm this parallel situation Lowry subtly compares another reference to Faustus' predicament with the Consul's former plight. Faustus exclaims, "How! bell, book, and candle — candle, book, and bell — / Forward and backward, to curse Faustus to hell." Bell, book, and candle is the old ceremony of major excommunication. The bell announced this to all; the book represented authority; while the candle was believed to symbolize the possibility that the ban might be lifted by the repentance and amendment of its victim for, just as the candle was used and extinguished, so the excommunication itself might be. *Twelve* priests and a bishop all held lighted candles; the bishop recited the formula which ended:

> We separate him, together with his accomplices and abettors, from the precious body and blood of the Lord and from the society of all Christians; we exclude him from our holy mother, the Church in heaven and on earth; we declare him excommunicate and anathema; we judge him damned, with the Devil and his angels and all the reprobate, to eternal fire until he shall recover himself from the toils of the Devil and return to amendment and to penitence.

Those present answered, "So be it!" The candles were extinguished by being dashed on the ground. The ceremony ended. Laruelle's misquotation of "fly" for "run" is due to the "elusive flickering candlelight"; finishing the letter he holds it into the candle flame until it is extinguished. Then, "suddenly from outside, a bell spoke out, then ceased abruptly: *dolente ... dolore!*" Again the ceremony has ended.

Geoffrey's affliction is drunkenness in its most compulsive and irremediable state. In the "Preface to a Novel" Lowry wrote, "on one level, the drunkenness of the Consul may be regarded as symbolizing the universal drunkenness of war, of the period that precedes war, no matter when." In his letter Geoffrey writes, "this is how I drink too, as if I were taking an eternal sacrament." It is essential to recall Faustus celebrating the sacrament of the Black Mass. Lowry certifies this intended analogy in the "Preface": "William James . . . might be in agreement with me when I affirm that the agonies of the drunkard find a very close parallel in the agonies of the mystic who has abused his powers." Indeed, in *The Varieties of Religious Experience,* James concludes a passage on this very subject with the statement that "The drunken consciousness is one bit of the mystic consciousness. . . ." Since Lowry also conceived of the drunken Consul as a universal symbol, the Faust theme expands to wide-ranging socio-political implications. In *The Decline of the West* Oswald Spengler characterized the spirit of modern Europe and America as Faustian, a condition which pictured man as ageing and wasted, but still hoping to comprehend and achieve everything, including the impossible. Nevertheless, western man, having become civilized, is effete, *infirm*, and defenceless, and therefore must perish. Visible then in the fall of Geoffrey is the fall of our Faustian civilization. Spengler, quoted by Hugh Firmin, Geoffrey's half-brother, is an important functional reference throughout *Under the Volcano.*

The symbolic importance of the frequent cinema advertisements for *Las Manos de Orlac* is due partially to the Faustian allusions in Maurice Renard's book, *The Hands of Orlac*, from which the film was adapted. Resine, the blonde wife of the pianist Stephen Orlac who, in an operation to save his hands, is given the hands of a supposed murderer, is haunted by a devil's head—a Mephisto—a Fantomo. Indeed, Yvonne refers to Geoffrey as a "phantom". For the Yvonne-like Rosine ". . . it was a partial and chance resemblance, inspired by the character in Faust." Stephen's studio, where he retains his hands for the piano, becomes "the Temple of Hands. Here were installed the two electric machines, the practise keyboard, and all the physical and chemical apparatus with which he had provided himself. And there were also some special books in a pile. The place soon looked like Dr. Faust's den." Like Faustus, who "surfeits upon cursed necromancy," Stephen also becomes interested in the subject: he observes that ". . . necromants or necromaticians make it a practice to evoke the dead so as to obtain by their aid some light upon the future." Lowry's entire technique of literary allusion has particularly this same purpose. Apart from common references to Baudelaire and to secret and occult books, two motifs of *The Hands of Orlac* also run through

Under the Volcano: "... from day to day he was slipping down into an abyss," and "the dead are coming back to life."

Into the third chapter Lowry introduces a pair of Faustian familiars who battle to direct Geoffrey's conscience. By definition, a familiar is a spirit supposed to attend and obey a sorcerer; also, in naming them "guardian angels" Lowry makes his allusion to Faustus' Good and Evil Angels obvious. The opening paragraph of this chapter includes a Faustus paraphrase: "Look up at that niche in the wall over there on the house where Christ is still, suffering, who would help you if you asked him: you cannot ask him." Faustus observes and does ask momentarily. "Ay, Christ, my Saviour,/ Seek to save distressed Faustus' soul!" The latter lines significantly follow the last pleas of both angels in the play. Likewise, Geoffrey's familiars do not finally abandon him until an hour before his end. The Evil Angel strikes first, urging the Consul to drink rather than think of Yvonne: "... the voice he recognized of a pleasant and impertinent familiar, perhaps horned, prodigal of disguise, a specialist in casuistry." The Good Angel angrily retorts: "Neither do I believe in the strychnine, you'll make me cry again, you bloody fool Geoffrey Firmin, I'll kick your face in, O idiot!" The "first familiar" wins this round as Geoffrey downs half the strychnine. The Good Angel threatens Geoffrey again, unsuccessfully. Both reappear before temporarily leaving the Consul, their battleground. The final reference to *Doctor Faustus* in this chapter comes when Geoffrey interjects, "please remind me to get back my Elizabethan plays."

Faust, as distinct from Dr. Faustus, is alluded to in this third chapter as Geoffrey thinks uneasily of "Goethe's famous church bell in pursuit of the child truant from church." Lowry has cleverly summarized Faust's soliloquy in which bells and voices in the Eastern Dawn prevent him from taking his life. Geoffrey and Faust are ironically juxtaposed; the former poisons his soul with each drink, while the latter is persuaded by a choir of angels, all Good, against self-destruction by poison. As a boy, Faust strayed in fields and forests but was always entranced by the sabbath bells. Their sounds now help prevent him from committing suicide. Geoffrey, however, is hardened against such precautions: "Goethe's church bell was looking him straight between the eyes; fortunately, he was prepared for it." Before conquering his despair Faust had cried, "I hear, but lack the faith, am dispossessed." Similarly, Geoffrey has been referred to as a "poor, lonely dispossessed trembling soul." Both men recognize the soul's life-giving source, but only Faust aspires to seek it. Both men thirst after knowledge, but Geoffrey's unquenchable alcoholic thirst takes precedence in his case. At one time he had hoped to write a book on Atlantis, the main part of which was to be "the chapters on the alchemists." On this topic he refers to "the old alchemists of Prague . . . living among the cohabitations of Faust himself."

In chapter four, Bernal Diaz, William Blackstone, Geoffrey and Faustus are all employed to illustrate precisely a viewpoint noted by Spengler in *The Decline of the West*: "Dramas like that of the emigration to America — man by man, each on his own account, driven by deep promptings to loneliness, — or the Spanish Conquest, or the Californian gold-rush, dramas of uncontrollable longings for freedom, solitude, immense independence . . . these dramas are Faustian and only Faustian." Limitless space is the prime symbol of the Faustian soul. Thus, Geoffrey's paraphrase of Diaz, the author of *The Discovery and Conquest of Mexico 1517-1521*, and his wish to escape like Blackstone, are understandable. To quote Spengler again: "To fly, to free one's self from earth, to lose one's self in the expanse of the universe — is not this ambition Faustian in the highest degree?" Unfortunately, Mexico has been plagued by exploiters ever since Cortez and Diaz. Hugh remembers once hearing the potential solution: "For man, every man, Juan seemed to be telling him, even as Mexico, must ceaselessly struggle upward," a paraphrase of the novel's epigraph from *Faust*. This quotation is part of the song of the angels who bear the immortal remains of Faust to heaven. Man and the world must follow Juan's advice to achieve a final salvation similar to Faust's. Geoffrey, however, sleeps throughout the chapter, but retains his Faustian identity in the minds of Hugh and Yvonne. Hugh asks, "How much does he really know about all this alchemy and cabbala business? How much does it mean to him?," and even jokes, "Maybe he's a black magician!"

The Faustian familiars reappear in chapter five as Geoffrey awakens from his Indic dream with "demons gnattering in his ears." The evil one advises him to ". . . just take one drink, just the necessary, the therapeutic drink: perhaps two drinks," but before he does so another voice retorts, "Put that bottle down, Geoffrey Firmin, what are you doing to yourself?" "The emptiness in the air after filled with whispers: alas, alas. Wings it really meant." Geoffrey's last hours are literally flying away as, at the chapter's end the good familiar cries out in desperation, "Stop it, for God's sake, you fool. Watch your step. We can't help you any more."

The role of Geoffrey as a Faustian magician is strengthened by a quotation from Shelley's *Alastor*: "Twelve o'clock, and the Consul said to the doctor: 'Ah, that the dream of the dark magician in his visioned cave, even while his hand — that's the bit I like — shakes in its last decay, were the true end of this so lovely world." Lines 681-6 of *Alastor* read as follows:

31

> O, that the dream
> Of dark magician in his visioned cave,
> Raking the cinders of a crucible
> For life and power, even when his feeble hand
> Shakes in its last decay, were the true law
> Of this so lovely world!

The misquotation of "end" for "law" is a noteworthy Freudian slip since Geoffrey is inadvertently comparing the magician's last stages with his own and the world's, whereas Shelley does not imply that the death of the magician causes the world's end. He puns on the word "Katabasis" but the application of the term underlines the present predicament. This *is* a descent into the nether world, into an inferno. Indeed, the attempt to insert a katabasis into the second part of *Faust*, first as a descent to the Mothers, and then as the classical Walpurgis Night, was evidently one of the most baffling structural problems of that work, as well as being one of the most crucial sections of the play.

The familiars are mentioned by Geoffrey next in chapter seven: "As for the demons, they were inside him as well as outside; quiet at the moment — taking their siesta perhaps — he was none the less surrounded by them and occupied; they were in possession." In *Doctor Faustus* the evil demons appear as the Seven Deadly Sins. Faustus's line, "O, I'll leap up to my God! — Who pulls me down?" seems to be applicable to a momentarily penitent Geoffrey when "the weight of a great hand seemed to be pressing his head down." Jacques disparagingly compares Marlowe's sense of perspective to Geoffrey's: "Christopher Marlowe, your Faust man, saw the Carthaginians fighting on his big toe-nail. That's the kind of clear seeing you indulge in. Everything seems perfectly clear, in terms of the toe-nail." Ironically, the analogy gives great compliment to Geoffrey's powers of vision. He remarks, "It was already the longest day in his entire experience, a life-time," when a few lines earlier the pun *Dies Faustus* had appeared. Marlowe's Faustus loved knowledge and power more than he did Christ, while Goethe's Faust would have reached the same tragic end were it not for the love of Margareta who brings him salvation. Geoffrey's fate fluctuates between these two poles. His potential saviour, Yvonne, first dreamed of making a new start with Geoffrey in British Columbia on Lake Pineaus where he owned an island. Coincidental or not, in *Faust: Part Two* the lower Peneus is a similar lotusland Eden.

In chapter ten the personal and the political are two main frames of reference. Spengler's observation on this point is helpful: "There are two sorts of Destiny, two sorts of war, two sorts of tragedy — public and private. Nothing can eliminate this duality from the world." As a private individual and as a public representative, the Consul symbolically portrays an ambivalent character; a Faust figure and an Everyman figure simultaneously. He uses one of Marlowe's most famous lines as a point of departure. Looking at Cervantes' prize-fighting cock he asks, "Was this the face that launched five hundred ships, and betrayed Christ into being in the Western Hemisphere?" In Conrad Aiken's *Blue Voyage*, an important literary source for parts of *Under the Volcano*, the main character, Demarest, had used this same line for his own comic points of departure: "Is this the face that scuttled a thousand ships?" Chapter ten concludes with Geoffrey voicing a Faustus-like frustration. Into the oncoming storm he cries out, "I love hell. I can't wait to get back there. In fact I'm *running*. I'm almost back there already." Faustus's soul was divided between a desire for mastery and a sense of guilt. Geoffrey despairingly envisions a comparable dichotomy: "What is man but a little soul holding up a corpse?" Like Faustus, he is tragic because he recognizes this dilemma as real. As Faustus boasts that his soul is his own to dispose of as he will, he hears the fearful echoes thundering in his ears. Similarly, as Geoffrey proclaims his love of hell there is also a contradictory emendation, for, "the queer thing was, he wasn't quite serious." Nature forewarns Geoffrey, just as it did Faustus: "Before him the volcanoes, precipitous, seemed to have drawn nearer. They towered up over the jungle, into the lowering sky — massive interests moving up in the background."

A letter from Lowry to his American editor, Albert Erskine, July 15, 1946 shows Lowry's concern with *Faust* in chapter eleven. Remembering Julian Green's note in his *Diary* to end a book with the image of the heroine rising to heaven, Lowry added to this idea one contained in the opera *Faust* when Margareta rises to heaven while Faust descends to hell. Thus, the simultaneous actions of Yvonne and Geoffrey in chapters eleven and twelve parallel the splitting of the path as two roads diverge into the Mexican wood to two opposing destinies.

Geoffrey's last hour commences when he sees "a clock pointing to six." The Faustian parallel of the last hour permits an ironic contrast. After the clock strikes eleven, Faustus, aware of impending damnation, exclaims, "Now hast thou but one bare hour to live./And then thou must be damned perpetually!" Through an almost fatalistic determinism, Geoffrey's approaching death is similarly inevitable. He, however, apathetically accepts the end, totally lacking Faustus's frantic longing for life. Yet Geoffrey's death is fully in accord with Spengler's theory of the determinism of inevitable decline for the Faustian spirit of western man in the twentieth century, the death of modern man, as Jung put it, in search of his soul.

Asking "What is a lost soul?" Geoffrey, in answering himself, describes himself: "It is one that has turned from its true path and is groping in the darkness of remembered ways."

Time ticks on: "the ticking of his watch, his heart, his conscience, a clock somewhere." In vain Faustus ordered, "Stand still, you ever-moving spheres of heaven,/ That time may cease, and midnight never come." Geoffrey makes no such plea, but only notes and recalls while his familiars make their last supplications. He hears them argue, and then "the voices ceased." They return as "daemonic orchestras" and "insolent archfiends", and lastly come to him as he lies with Maria, the prostitute, "hissing and shrieking and yammering at him: 'Now you've done it, Geoffrey Firmin! Even we can help you no longer ... Just the same you might as well make the most of it now, the night's still young.' " Young it is, but for Geoffrey it is almost over. Even Maria is part of the Faustian tradition, for in ancient Coptic manuscripts the magician and the prostitute played an equal role to that of the magician and the virgin, Yvonne in this case. Now, at six-thirty, "A bell clanged frantically in the distance" just as for Faustus the clock strikes the half-hour. Spengler wrote that, "Besides the clock, the bell itself is a Western 'symbol'." As such it is a Faustian symbol as well.

The crag of the Malebolge reminds Geoffrey of Shelley's *The Cenci*, Coleridge's *Kubla Klan*, and Calderon. The last reference is probably to Calderon de la Barca's play *The Wonder-Working Magician*, to whose Faust theme Goethe was indebted. The play opens in a wood where Cyprian and a Demon argue about the unity of God. Cyprian later sells his soul for Justina, his beloved. The two die on the scaffold and ascend to heaven. The following lines from Calderon's play depict imagery visible also in the Malebolge: "Though from that proud height you fall/ Headlong down a dark abyss"; "Abyss of hell, prepare,/ Yourself the region of your own despair!" and especially the following lines:

> This mountain's brow is bound
> With curling mist, like streaming hair
> Spread out below, and all the horizon round
> Is one volcanic pyre!

Geoffrey describes the sunset as "A mercurochrome agony down the west". The suggestion of a blood-red crucifixion is comparable to the description by Faustus: "See, see, where Christ's blood streams in the firmament!/ One drop would save my soul, half a drop," a parallel that occurs elsewhere as I have already indicated, one year later, as a "gigantic red evening, whose reflection bled

away in the deserted swimming pools." Faustus's futile plea for even half a drop
is paralleled in Geoffrey's thirst: "the thirst that was not thirst, but itself heart-
break, and lust, was death, death, and death again." He remembers once carrying
a carafe of water in the hotel *El Infierno* but unable to put it to his lips he hears
a voice saying "you cannot drink of it," and believes "it must have been Jesus
who sent me this." The comparable line in *Doctor Faustus* is "Ah, rend not my
heart for naming of my Christ!" Meanwhile we hear "the clock ticking forward"
with Geoffrey abandoning "The hope of any new life together, even were it
miraculously offered again."

Reflecting on "that extraordinary picture on Laruelle's wall, *Los Borrachones*,"
Geoffrey applies the book's epigraph from Faust to himself:

> When he had striven upwards as at the beginning with Yvonne, had not the
> "features" of life seemed to grow more clear, more animated, friends and enemies
> more identifiable, special problems, scenes, and with them the sense of his own
> reality, more *separate* from himself? And had it not turned out that the farther
> down he sank, the more those features had tended to dissemble, to cloy and clutter,
> to become finally little better than ghastly caricatures of his dissimulating inner
> and outer self, or of his struggle, if struggle there were still?

In his descent, his katabasis, Geoffrey becomes a corporate and composite character, incorporating all damned souls, just as with successive masks he has been all
of the literary models alluded to, a timeless Everyman. He joins the "downward
flight" of souls beyond salvation, just as Yvonne has already joined the ascending
flight, à la Margareta, although her death follows Geoffrey's.

Time moves on, "One, two, three, four, five, twelve, six, seven." Geoffrey's
last twelve hours conclude in this twelfth chapter at seven o'clock. "The clock
outside quickly chimed seven times." As the clock for Faustus strikes twelve,
thunder and lightning ensue. Similarly, "Thunderclaps crashed on the mountains
and then at hand," and "Lightning flashed like an inch-worm going down the
sky." "A bell spoke out: *dolente . . . dolore!*" Faust and Dante are again echoed
in this tolling, just as they are combined one year later for Jacques. It is Geoffrey's
passing bell, his funeral bell, but it also tolls for everyman.

Even the horse who, escaping from the clutching hands of Geoffrey, gallops
uncontrollably through the forest to kill Yvonne, is ironically anticipated by
Faustus' line, itself a quotation from Ovid's *Amores*, "*O lente, lente currite, noctis
equi*," but time and the horse wait for no man. Just as Faustus cries "O, I'll leap
up to my God! — Who pulls me down?" Geoffrey experiences a similar prevention
of his attempt upward: "He raised his head again; no, he was where he was,

there was nowhere to *fly* to. And it was as if a black dog had settled on his back, pressing him to his seat." Similarly, Faustus has nowhere to fly to. He pleads, "Mountains and hills, come, come, and fall on me,/ And hide me from the heavy wrath of God!" Likewise, Geoffrey deliriously deludes himself that in the Himalayas, imaged by Popocatepetl, is a final resting place. Carrying "the Hotel Fausto's information" in his pocket, he mentally attempts to climb the volcano, as his father had climbed the Himalayas. Faustus had also hoped to be borne aloft to heaven in the volcano's breath:

> Now draw up Faustus, like a foggy mist,
> Into the entrails of yon labouring clouds,
> That, when you vomit forth into the air,
> My limbs may issue from your smoky mouths,
> So that my soul may but ascend to heaven!

Goethe presents a similar hell intended for Faust:

> out from the arching jaw
> A raging swill of fiery flood is spewed;
> See, in the seething fume of that dread maw,
> The town of flames eternally renewed.
> Up to the teeth, the molten red comes rushing,
> The damned swim wildly, hoping to be saved,
> Then, where the huge hyena's jaws are crushing,
> Renew their path with burning brimstone paved.

"Somebody threw a dead dog after him down the ravine." Bunyan and Faustus come instantaneously to mind. In the Bunyan epigraph to *Under the Volcano* the dog's soul is not doomed to perish in Hell as is man's, yet man must die like an animal. The pariah dog, a symbol of guilt, has followed Geoffrey throughout the book, and even earlier in this last chapter is still associated with his fate: "And it was as if a black dog had settled on his back, pressing him to his seat" as I have quoted above. As an outcast of society Geoffrey is a pariah.

Suggestions of a cyclical reincarnation are latent in chapter one. Vigil talks of sunset when begin "all the dogs to shark." When Laruelle is in the cinema "Dark shapes of pariah dogs prowled in and out of the stalls." Lastly, talking to Laruelle, Sr. Bustamente, the cinema manager, refers to Geoffrey as "the *bicho*, the one with the blue eyes." Certainly, Laruelle is haunted by the spiritual ghosts of Yvonne and Geoffrey, if not also by a physical embodiment of each. Faustus wished to be reincarnated to escape damnation. Finally, in lines that Bunyan might well have known and paraphrased, Faustus cries:

Why wert thou not a creature wanting soul?
Or why is this immortal that thou hast?
Ah, Pythagoras' metempsychosis, were that true,
This soul should *fly* from me and I be chang'd
Unto some brutish beast! all beasts are happy,
For, when they die,
Their souls are soon dissolv'd in elements;
But mine must live still to be plag'd in hell.

Employing the Faust archetype, Lowry has achieved the sense of ironic dissimilarity and yet of profound human continuity between the modern protagonist and his long dead exemplars; he has also locked past and present together spatially in a timeless unity by transmuting the time-world of history into the timeless world of myth, the common content of modern literature.

(1965)

UNDER SEYMOUR MOUNTAIN

A Note on Lowry's Stories

George Woodcock

MALCOLM LOWRY was born in England in 1909. He died there in 1957. And during the restless life that stretched between those poles of destiny he wandered over a great portion of the earth — the Far East, the United States, much of Europe, and, of course, Mexico, the setting of his now belatedly celebrated novel, *Under the Volcano*. But almost a third of his life — and the most productive third so far as his writing was concerned — he spent in Canada. He came to Vancouver just before the war, in 1939, and the next year settled in a squatter's cabin on the foreshore of Burrard Inlet at Dollarton, a settlement under the shadow of the mountains, a few miles east of Vancouver. There, with time off for trips back to Mexico and Europe and Eastern Canada, he lived until 1954, when he left for Sicily and, finally, England.

It was at Dollarton, and at Niagara-on-the-Lake, that Lowry finished the last, published version of *Under the Volcano*. It was at Dollarton also that he wrote the stories which are published in the volume entitled *Hear Us O Lord From Heaven Thy Dwelling Place*. He worked at the same time on at least two novels about Mexico, *La Mordida* and *Dark as the Grave*, of which, so far as I know, only fragments remain among the great mass of manuscript material that has recently been assembled at the University of British Columbia. Among that material is also — apart from enough poems to make a considerable volume — the almost completed manuscript of a novel, *October Ferry to Gabriola*, which is set in British Columbia, and which also will be published as soon as the editing is complete.[1]

[1] *Dark as the Grave Wherein my Friend Is Laid* and *October Ferry to Gabriola* have since been edited and published, and essays on them appear in this volume. ED.

I do not think there is much doubt that Lowry has one foot well in the realm of Canadian literature. It is not merely that on Canadian soil he produced the final, magnificent version of what many critics regard as the best novel written in our land; nor is it merely that much of his later work was set in Canada. We do not, after all, regard D. H. Lawrence as anything but an English writer, though he wrote many of his books abroad and set them in foreign countries. Try as he might to escape from his past, Lawrence remained the travelling Englishman, refracting all he saw through a personal and alien eye; his best writing on other lands was prompted by the lyrical observations of an outsider, and when he tried to enter into the heart of Mexico and portray it from within, he produced that literary monstrosity, *The Plumed Serpent*.

Lowry's relationship to his adopted home was quite different. We read the poems he wrote on Burrard Inlet; we read the three Canadian stories in *Hear Us O Lord From Heaven Thy Dwelling Place* — "The Bravest Boat", "Gin and Golden Rod", particularly "The Forest Path to the Spring". And we realize that he is not in fact writing about Canada as a transient outsider. He is writing about it as a man who over fifteen years lived himself into the environment that centred upon his fragile home where the Pacific tides lapped and sucked under the floorboards, and who identified himself with that environment — despite trials of flesh and spirit — as passionately as those other strangers who have rendered so well the essence of their particular corners of Canada, Frederick Philip Grove and Roderick Haig-Brown. If Mexico stirred him through that combination of antagonism and attraction which so many Europeans feel there, Canada — or at least that fragment of it which stretches out from Burrard Inlet to embrace the Gulf of Georgia — stirred him through a sympathy that led towards total involvement.

It is for this reason, perhaps, that in his Canadian stories the Websterian hell of *Under the Volcano* never comes to view, though one gets a whiff of the sulphur in "Gin and Goldenrod". No man goes down to destruction under Seymour Mountain, and along the beaches of Dollarton the phantoms with death's-head faces do not sing in the voices of demons as they did for Consul Firmin. On the contrary, here, in this closely and lovingly described land-and-inletscape, there is a sense of redemption; in "The Forest Path to the Spring" the mountain lion who sits in a tree over the path and embodies destruction runs away from the narrator's steady eye, and what the latter remembers about his trips to the spring — what he remembers most vividly — is the almost mystical experience of joy that at times seemed to carry him in a rhapsodic instant from the life-giving source back to the door of his cabin. Here, as in *Under the Volcano*, the self is immersed. But in the novel it drowns in the whirlpool of self-negation, whereas in "The Forest Path to the Spring" it bathes in a universal calm, the calm of a world of nature as sympathetic as ever Wordsworth wrote of, with which it identifies and from which it returns with joy enriched. It seems to me that it is in this almost rhapsodic identification with place that we find our best reason to claim much of what Lowry wrote for the literature of Canada. For it is not a sense of place that derives from mere observation, like that conveyed by a sensitive and competent travel writer; it is rather the sense of place that derives from a mental naturalization which adds to a native's sense of identity the wonder of newness a native can never experience fully after childhood.

The stories in *Hear Us O Lord From Heaven Thy Dwelling Place* are all worth reading for themselves; some of the non-Canadian examples, while they do not attain the intensity of feeling of "The Forest Path to the Spring", are interesting for their experimental exploration of the problems of conveying multiple levels of meaning. "Through the Panama" is an example; the narrator, a transmuted Lowry figure, voyages to Europe by freighter, but his journey is also that of a modern Ancient Mariner, with the albatross of literary creation and its attendant curse hung around his neck as he considers his novels about novelists who are his own mirror images. For Lowry belonged in the early twentieth century cosmopolitan tradition that seemed to reach an end about the time of his death — the tradition of Proust and Gide, which came to the conclusion, inevitable after a century of introspection, that the proper study of the writer is the writer's mind.

But all these stories are also part of a great continuum, a vast Work in Progress that filled Lowry's life and was never completed — perhaps never could be completed. In this sense Lowry was of the Proustian rather than of the Gidian tradition. The Gidians write many separate studies of experience, all related, but each self-contained; when one novel is finished a phase of investigation is ended, its record is terminated as quickly as possible, and then the writer is on to the next experience and the next novel. But the Proustians, and Lowry among them, conceive all their work as one great inter-related pattern on whose parts they work continuously and simultaneously. Proust could never leave the one great work of his life alone; he worked backwards and forwards over his manuscript, and only publication ever gave a final form to any of its parts; only death, one can be sure, put a period to the work itself, coming by coincidence at the point when Proust had reached the end of his original plan. So it was with Lowry.

He worked on several novels, on stories and poems, all at the same time, and his revisions were multiple to the point of Flaubertian obsession. For this reason he spent many years over each novel, writing on others at the same time; his actually completed works are few out of all proportion to those he sketched out and started. Another decade of work might — and equally well might not — have presented us with a masterpiece in its own very different way rivalling *À la Recherche du temps perdu*, perhaps even in one direction exceeding it, since Lowry possessed no cork-lined room and revised and added to his Work in Progress as the result, not of remembering a past now dead, but of experiencing and incorporating a lived present.

As it is, when *October Ferry to Gabriola* is published and the devoted labours of Lowry's editors have salvaged all that is publishable in fragmentary form from the other portions of the great cycle, we shall perhaps begin to see, at least in massive outlines, the modern Divine Comedy of which *Under the Volcano*, for all its portentous self-sufficiency, was intended only as a part.

(1961)

DEATH IN LIFE

Neo-Platonic Elements in
"Through the Panama"

Geoffrey Durrant

THE EXPLORATION of Malcolm Lowry's symbolism will no doubt occupy scholars for many years; in this field at least we are offered "God's plenty". What I suggest in this article is meant as a mere footnote to such studies as Perle Epstein's of the influence of the Cabbala, and as a suggestion for possible further investigations.[1]

To a reader who is familiar with the literature of neo-Platonism it seems likely that at times Malcolm Lowry is drawing on a system of symbols derived not only from general Cabbalistic lore, but from more particular sources in the neo-Platonic tradition. In this tradition, as it is represented by the work of such writers as Proclus, Porphyry, Apuleius and Claudianus, the Platonic view of the world as a cave of darkness is united with the Greek and Roman pantheons, and with Homer, to create a philosophical mythology — a mythology in which the fate of Psyche, of Persephone, of Narcissus and of Ulysses is understood as an allegory of the descent of the soul into the world of the senses — the dark wood or the dark sea of matter. The principal English source for this material is to be found in the writings of Thomas Taylor the Platonist; this is in part now made widely accessible through the publication of a selection of his writings by Kathleen Raine and George Mills Harper.[2]

Before proceeding to an examination of one of Malcolm Lowry's stories to illustrate this suggestion, it is necessary to point out that in the neo-Platonic system of myths the soul has its true home in the heavens; through an error it falls in love with its own generated image, and proceeds into generation. That is to say, it is born into this world of darkness, where its task is to purify itself of the material grossness which encloses it, and to ascend through the elements to the heavenly region of the stars — the true home from which it has been exiled. The journey of the soul is variously represented as the flight of a bird, a voyage over the dark sea of matter, or a fall into dark waters. The life of the senses is represented as *entrapment* in a web, a dark wood, or a cave. The stars are a constant reminder of the life that has been lost through generation, or birth, since the stars to which we look up are souls that enjoy the divine life of the heavens. We yearn, like Coleridge's Ancient Mariner, "towards the journeying Moon and the stars"; the Moon is regarded in this philosophy as the sphere of judgement, the staging post between the divine and the fallen worlds, since the sphere of the moon marks the limits of the world of generation.

Malcolm Lowry's story "Through the Panama"[3] evidently has an eschatological significance, and a gloss from "The Ancient Mariner" is there used as a comment on this statement:

> ... And later, the stars: but now Martin saw the fixity of the closed order of their system: death in short. The thought comes from Keyserling. (They are *not dead* when I looked at them with Primrose.) Wonderful truth in Lawrence about this. "Somehow my life draws (he writes) strength from the depths of the universe, from the depths among the stars, from the great world!"

The gloss from Coleridge is as follows:

> In his loneliness and fixedness the Ancient Mariner yearneth towards the journeying Moon, and the stars that still sojourn, yet still move onward; and everywhere the blue sky belongs to them, and is their appointed rest and their native country and their own natural home, which they enter unannounced, as guests that are certainly expected, and yet there is a silent joy at their arrival.

As we shall see, the journey to the south and again to the north is itself a representation, in the neo-Platonic system, of the myth of a fall by generation, or birth, into the world of the senses, and of the long voyage home to the native land, the paternal port of the soul. The inclusion of this gloss in an evidently eschatological account of a voyage suggests strongly that Lowry understood "The Ancient Mariner" as drawing upon a related eschatology — a view which, given Coleridge's early interest in the neo-Platonists and in the work of Thomas Taylor, is by no means to be dismissed as absurd.

In the neo-Platonic interpretation of the voyage of Ulysses, the life of man on earth is represented as the voyage of the intellect over the dark sea of matter; the ship represents the body, the sailors the human faculties, and Ulysses the intellect.[4] Exiled from his true home, or natal port, Ulysses is assailed by many temptations, and finally returns to his paternal home, where he is united with Penelope, the true wisdom, and is once more at peace.[5] Closely associated with this myth, in Thomas Taylor's account, is that of the Cave of the Nymphs, for which the chief source is also in Porphyry. Here the cave represents the world of the senses; it has two gates, one towards the north and the other to the south. It is through the northern gate or 'port' that souls descend into the cave, and through the southern that they ascend to heaven:

> From among the number of these [signs] the theologists consider Cancer and Capricorn as two ports; Plato calls them two gates. Of these, they affirm that Cancer is the gate through which souls descend, but Capricorn that through which they ascend, and exchange a material for a divine condition of being. Cancer, indeed, is northern and adapted to descent: but Capricorn is southern, and accommodated to ascent.[6]

These two accounts are not fused into one by Porphyry, or by Taylor, though Taylor originally published his version of Porphyry's *Voyage of Ulysses* as a footnote of great length to his translation of *Concerning the Cave of the Nymphs*; this footnote refers immediately to the following sentence in that work:

> Indeed it appears to me that it was not without foundation that Numenius thought that the person of Ulysses in the Odyssey represented to us a man who passes in a regular manner over the dark and stormy sea of generation.[7]

When these two closely related interpretations of Homer are taken together, they produce a myth in which the human spirit embarks through a port or gate on a southerly voyage on the dark sea of matter, descends to imprisonment in the Hades of the senses in the extreme south, and then proceeds northwards to the port or gate of the north, where it may hope to escape from its long and stormy exile. There are I believe strong indications that "Through the Panama" is deliberately coloured with suggestions of this myth, and moreover that Lowry interpreted "The Ancient Mariner" as an expression of the same myth.

In "Through the Panama" the port of departure is Vancouver; in the neo-Platonic myth it is the port or gate of birth, through which the soul enters the dark sea of matter. The ship is the *Diderot* — a vessel of "enlightenment"; its engines sing "Frère Jacques" to awaken the intellect. (There is a paradox here only on the surface, for it is only through the life of the intellect that the ship may hope to arrive at its true destination.) The birth imagery is unobtrusive; midnight and mud are traditional symbols of generation:

> Leaving Vancouver, British Columbia, Canada, midnight, November 7th, 1947, S.S. *Diderot*, for Rotterdam.
> Rain, rain and dark skies all day.
> We arrive at dusk, in a drizzle. Everything wet, dark, slippery . . .

(This morning, walking through the forest, a moment of intense emotion: the path sodden, a morass of mud, and sad dripping trees and ocherous fallen leaves; here it all is. I cannot believe I won't be walking down the path tomorrow.)

The use of Stanley Park and Dollarton as versions of Paradise is evident enough in two other stories in this volume — "The Bravest Boat" and "The Forest Path to the Spring"; here the paradise is lost as the voyager prepares to set out on his journey.

The journey to the south begins:

... The black cloudy sky was breaking and stars were brilliant overhead. The Northern Cross. November 8th. High salt wind, clear blue sky, hellishly rough sea (zig-zagged with a lashing rip tide) through the Juan de Fuca Strait. — Whale geometry of Cape Flattery: finny phallic furious face of Flattery.

The generation theme is evident here, not only in the obvious phallicism, but also in the strong wind and the "hellishly rough sea" under the sign of the North. Porphyry, in Taylor's version of *The Cave of the Nymphs*, writes:

Indeed, Boreas (the North Wind) is proper to souls passing into generation: for the northern blasts recreate those who are on the verge of death ... For the north, from its superior coldness, collects into one, detains and strengthens the soul in the most moist and frigid embraces of terrene generation. ...[8]

(Here it may be noted that the Ancient Mariner is blown southward by the northern storm-blast, which is "tyrannous and strong". The similarity here and elsewhere suggests that there is a close relationship between Lowry's story and Coleridge's poem.) That the sea is "hellishly rough" is only the first example of Lowry's use, in an apparently offhand way, of conversational expressions that are meant to carry a considerable weight of significance. Since, in the neo-Platonic philosophy, this world is Hades or Hell, the sea that represents the world of the senses is indeed "hellish".

The condition of the exiled soul is that of alienation:

This desolate sense of alienation possibly universal sense of dispossession. The cramped cabin one's obvious place on earth.

At Los Angeles another passenger is taken on: "His name? Charon. Naturally." The voyage to the south continues, and the hellish desolation increases:

Strange islands, barren as icebergs, and nearly as white. Rocks! — The Lower California Coast, giant pinnacles, images of barrenness and desolation, on which the heart is thrown and impaled eternally.

In "The Ancient Mariner" the journey to the south brings the Mariner to the desolation of a world of ice. Lowry cannot directly use this in a voyage to the Panama Canal; but he can see the likeness of guano-covered islands to icebergs, and so continue the relationship with Coleridge that is made explicit first in the stories of the attempt to shoot an albatross and the saving of a man's life by an albatross. In the increasing desolation of the southward voyage, the song of the *Diderot's* engines, which awakened the mind to consciousness and adventure, now turns to a lament. The voyage has led this Ulysses into the shadow of spiritual death; the albatross of salvation is replaced by the digarilla, "a bird of ill omen". As rational consciousness awakens, man becomes imprisoned in his world:

> Man not enmeshed by, but *killed* by his own book and the malign forces it arouses. Wonderful theme. Buy planchette for necessary dictation.
> — Death takes a holiday. On a Liberty ship.
> — Or does he? All day I hear him "cackling like a pirate."

The voyage of enlightenment and liberty, with the S.S. *Diderot* headed for the south — the world of material things — is a journey to spiritual death; the soul has been entrapped:

> ...I am a voice, yet with physical feelings, I enter what can only be described — I won't describe it — with teeth, that snap tight behind me: at the same time, in an inexplicable way, this is like going through the Panama Canal, and what closes behind me is, as it were, a lock: in a sense I am now a ship, but I am also a voice and also Martin Trumbaugh, and now I am, or he is, in the realm of death.... Death himself is a hideous looking red-faced keeper of a prison....

The world of 'reality' as a trap, a death-in-life, a prison; this is centrally in the neo-Platonic tradition. That the human being is "a ship" is also, as we have seen, one of the traditional myths of the neo-Platonists.

IN THIS WORLD, consciousness, as for the Ancient Mariner, is a hellish condition, since the love of life is lost. Here Lowry's gloss from "The Ancient Mariner" indicates a death-in-life: "And envieth that they should live, and so many lie dead." However, the ordeals that Ulysses undergoes are preparations and testings of the soul, and Lowry sees even this state of alienation and grief as an ordeal that can be miraculously overcome:

Sigbjørn Wilderness (pity my name is such a good one because I can't use it) could only pray for a miracle, that miraculously some love of life would come back.

It has: apparently this retracing of a course was part of the main ordeal; and even at this time Martin knew it to be no dream, but some strange symbolism of the future.

The crew of this ship will not mutiny, because "(a) this is a happy ship" and "(b) they want to be home for Christmas." The symbolism here is accompanied by praise of the French and is followed by the Captain's refusal to shoot the albatross that appears "crucified on the cross-trees." The *Diderot*, it seems, represents the kind of enlightenment that is not necessarily or permanently at war with the human senses and faculties, but gives them happiness in the prospect of "home". At the same time the Captain has reverence for life and for the principle of salvation represented by the Albatross-Christ. There is, it may be, a suggestion of brotherhood in liberty in the repeated use of "Frère Jacques" in this story; certainly at the end it appears as an expression of the enlightenment of love.

The Panama Canal itself is presented, through the device of a historical gloss in the margins, as the achievement of a "great new era of enlightenment" and as a technological realization of the modern spirit. In the traveller's personal experience, however, the Canal is the most hellish part of the journey:

> Blackest history of canal's horror, failure, collapse, murder, suicide, fever, at Calabra Cut.... Hot here as a Turkish bath in hell. Jungle has to be chopped back every day.

The *Diderot* is travelling to the eastern world (in Porphyry the abode of gods) while the *Manatee*, from London, is going to the western world (the abode, in Porphyry, of demons):[9]

> Another ship from London, all going the other way steaming very swiftly as with the current. (Bergson)

The British ship, as opposed to the French, is travelling with the current of history, and, as the gloss suggests, learning nothing of the madness of the westward journey to daemonic mechanical achievement:

> ...You would scarcely credit that so many people for so many years during this long era of enlightenment could be so goddamned stupid, could be so ferociously ignorant, could have learned so little, that they went on doing precisely this same sort of bloody thing.

47

The emergence of the *Diderot* from the last lock of the Canal offers an end to the fear of separation, or alienation, from Primrose:

And ourselves, watching, happy, happy at the news we won't be separated after all.

As I shall show, this apparently casual comment conveys, or attempts to convey, the happiness of the watchful and awakened mind at the knowledge of its union with the soul.

The journey to the north-east is still perilous, but Charon has been dropped, and the wine (pinard) and the cake indicate the sacramental hope that at the same time demands a sacrifice, and is therefore threatening:

But what is that cake going to demand of the Trumbaughs? The cake itself seems a nightmare. In spite of stars, wind, and sun, Martin had almost foundered in some complicated and absurd abyss of self, could only pray for another miracle to get out of it.

In the late classical eschatology, the journey of the soul to its heavenly home is achieved through a process of purgation, in which it is washed by rain, blown by the wind, and tormented by lightning, so that it is purified by the elements of water, air, and fire.[10] Lowry duly brings this in:

Two squalls; cobalt thunderstorms. Wind catches spray and blows it across the sea like rain, a tiny squall of rain.
Martin was gloomy and savage, lying all day in his bunk predicting death and disaster.
During these last days, since going through the Anageda Passage, have been through some important spiritual passage too — what does it mean?

"What it means" is that the soul is being cured of its attachment to material things, and is passing through its purgatorial ordeal.

Terrific squall towards sunset. Thunder. Cobalt lightnings reveal a sizzling sea . . . *vision of creation.*
— Am glad to be welcomed by skipper again — really believe I have now gone through some spiritual ordeal . . . though a little hard to see what.

The voyage into the Atlantic takes the ship into a "godawful storm"; the term is not to be taken lightly, for the wind that blows from the south is the terrible wind of God that blows souls out of generation into the true life after death, the equivalent of the "good south wind" that blows the Ancient Mariner northwards. The fear of death is evoked by Lowry in the passages for translation into French where "the man was not dead but his wife told him he had died two days ago"; and "she dressed herself as the Goddess of Death." This is the "King Storm whose sheen is Fearful." The terror of death is further heightened by the Conradian description of the storm, where the gloss from Coleridge adds the suggestion of a metaphysical terror:

> He heareth sounds, and seeth strange sights and commotions in the sky and the elements.

The religious dread is continued in the Rilke quotation from the Blessed Angela:

> ... "Si [Dieu] ... ne me changeait pas moi-même, s'il ne commençait au fond de moi une nouvelle operation, au lieu de me faire du bien, les sages, les saints et Dieu exaspéraient au delà de toute expression mon desespoir, ma fureur, ma tristesse, ma douleur, et mon aveuglement!"

The meaning of the wind that blows the soul northward with a terrible speed into the new birth of death is to be found in the classical eschatology:

> ... The southern gales dissolve life. ... the south (wind) is more vehement towards the end.[11]

Cicero records the speed of the soul as it leaves its corporeal nature:

> Add that the soul comes to make its escape all the more readily from our air ... because there is nothing swifter than the speed of the soul; there is no sort of speed which can match the speed of the soul.[12]

In Lowry, the gale gets steadily worse; and the climax is reached off the Azores; here Lowry uses Coleridge's gloss:

> The Mariner hath been cast into a trance; for the angelic power causeth the vessel to drive northward faster than human life could endure.

In spite of the realistic trappings, and the apparently leisurely discussion of literature and life, the intention is evidently to represent the terror of death. Lowry here permits himself a little joke:

> We have had to change our course, the skipper says, and are going by dead reckoning.

The storm at sea is paralleled by the storm in Martin's soul; on the northward and eastward voyage he searches his conscience, and undergoes a kind of purgation:

> Now you see how easy it is to be carried away by an impulse of hatred! There is some truth in what I say (that is, it is certainly true that I hate these people) but what of the whole thing, read aright? What testimony to my inadequacy, my selfishness, my complete confusion indeed!

49

The self-examination and the moral anguish in Martin's experience provide the natural counterpart of the elemental purging by wind, rain, and lightning. Doubt and fear assail the soul; the story about being thought to be the author of *The Trial,* and the claim to have recognized Kierkegaard before he was well known, are not mere anecdotes:

> The author . . . feels himself to be some sort of unrecognized pioneer, who maybe even lives himself in a state of Fear and Trembling, perhaps even in undergoing some sort of Trial at the moment.

In this situation Martin somewhat surprisingly turns not to beatific visions or a sense of sin, but to well-established Pythagorean and neo-Platonic virtues:

> Equilibrium, sobriety, moderation, wisdom: these unpopular and unpleasant virtues, without which meditation and even goodness are impossible, must somehow, because they are so unpleasant, be recommended as states of being to be embraced with a kind of passion.

These virtues are those recommended by the neo-Platonists, as a preparation for vision of the beautiful:

> Indeed, as the ancient oracle declares, temperance and fortitude, prudence and every virtue are certain purgatives of the soul.[13]

It is not surprising, then, to find Lowry ending this passage with a Pythagorean insistence on the unity of being, and the need for love, not only of men, but "of all God's creatures, human and animal".

The promise of reconciliation and release is offered in the memory of a French movie of *The Fall of the House of Usher*:

> . . . The unspeakably happy ending of the film, by the way, Martin thought, under the stars, with Orion suddenly turned into a cross, and Usher reconciled with his wife in this life yet on another plane, was a stroke of genius perhaps beyond Poe himself.

The significance given here to the appearance of Orion as the cross reflects the use of pagan myth mixed with Christian doctrine. The theme of union and separation is important in the story, and seems to reflect a modification of the attainment by Ulysses, in the myth, of union with his Penelope, the true wisdom of the soul. Of this Porphyry, in Taylor's account, tells us:

> . . . Ulysses will not always wish in vain for a passage over the dark ocean of a corporeal life, but by the assistance of Mercury, who may be considered as the emblem of reason, he will at length be enabled to quit the magic embraces of

Calypso, the goddess of Sense, and to return again into the arms of Penelope, or Philosophy, the long lost and proper object of his love.[11]

Martin's voyage, unlike that of Ulysses, begins in union with his true love, and only the entry into the Panama Canal — the hell of a rational and mechanical "enlightenment" — threatens him with separation from her: "Primrose and myself are the sole passengers aboard the freighter." The home they have left is, it seems, the true home of Primrose, who may be disquieted on the voyage if she is reminded of it:

"Keep quiet about house or will spoil voyage for Primrose."

Martin and Primrose are happy in their union within the ship:

Nov. 9. Primrose and Sigbjørn Wilderness are happy in their cramped Chief Gunner's cabin.

Primrose is the very source of living vision to Martin; "the stars are only *not dead* when I look at them with Primrose". Primrose is shown as characteristically responding to beauty and life:

A flying fish skidding over the sapphire sea toward an albatross floating to meet it: ecstasy. Primrose in seventh Heaven.

(This is clearly a symbolical passage, the flying-fish of the soul aspiring to the albatross of salvation.) It is only with the arrival at the Panama Canal that a separation is threatened:

Bad news: due to the unexpected arrival of more passengers in Cristobal, perhaps Primrose and I are to be separated, into different cabins.

However, even the Canal does not separate them, so that it seems that Lowry is claiming a unity through the darkest part of his journey with his Primrose or true wisdom of the soul. It is she who explains to him the significance of the locks:

Significance of *locks*: in each one you are locked, Primose says, as it were, in an experience.

The separation seems not to take place, though this is perhaps designedly not made quite clear in the story. After the voyage through the Canal the fear of separation is removed. It is Primrose who suggests the buying of wine. Primrose is "afraid of this boat, thrown together in wartime by makers of washing machines," a significant passage, since the soul is unhappy in the ship of the body, which is to undergo its purgation. Primrose is the principle to which Martin wishes to be true:

> Above all things perhaps he wanted to be loyal to Primrose in life. He wanted to be loyal to her beyond life, and in whatever life there might be beyond. He wanted to be loyal to her beyond death. In short, at the bottom of this chaos of a nature, he worshipped the virtues that the world seems long since to have dismissed as dull or simply good business or as not pertaining to reality at all. So that, as in his lower, so in his higher nature too, he felt himself to be non-human.

In this way Primrose is given the character of Martin's true soul, or wisdom. The saving of Primrose is, it seems, the concern of the ship's crew: "All night we have been saving your life Madame."

The presence of Martin's Primrose throughout the journey thus imposes an important modification of the Ulysses theme; but it does not represent a weakening of the neo-Platonic content. For to those familiar with the tradition in which Lowry is writing, Primrose is early in the story identified with Psyche, exiled from her starry home and threatened with separation from Cupid, her rational nature. In this way two different but related myths are interwoven in Lowry's story.

Of the myth of Psyche Taylor writes:

> Venus is represented desiring Mercury to proclaim Psyche through all lands, as one of her female slaves that has fled from her service.[15]

As the ship leaves Vancouver, the first mention of Primrose reveals her "wearing all her Mexican silver bracelets, calmly tense, electrically beautiful and excited". This is a slight but distinct hint of enslavement. When Primrose is next mentioned, Martin says he must "keep quiet about house or will spoil voyage for Primrose." The true home of Psyche or the soul is in Heaven, as Taylor records:

> [The descent of Psyche] signifies the descent of the soul from the intelligible world into a mundane condition of being, but without abandoning its establishment in the Heavens.[16]

This may be taken with the following passage in Taylor:

> The gems, too, on which Psyche is said to have trod in every part of the Palace [Heaven], are evidently symbolical of the stars.[17]

As the ship leaves Vancouver, the stars as jewels — the floor of Heaven — shine over the lovers as they set out on their southward journey:

> Leaving at night the jeweled city. Baguette of diamonds on black velvet, says

Primrose: ruby and emerald harbor lights. Topaz and gold lights on two bridges. Primrose is very happy. We embrace in the dark, on deck.

And later: "Our house. Incredible jewel-like days in December, sometimes."

The embrace "in the dark" evokes the love of Psyche for her Cupid, whom she was not allowed to see, and whom she loved in the dark. That she is "happy" is a reflection of the heavenly joy from which she is now departing on her exile, with its threat of separation. Psyche, according to Taylor, is tempted into the world of material things by her sisters, "imagination and nature", at the behest of Venus.[18] Throughout the story, Primrose is shown taking an eager interest and delight in nature, and an imaginative response to its life. Further, in the same passage, Taylor informs us that Psyche, after her descent, is "represented as having a stumbling and reeling gait," since "Plato, in the Phaedo, says, that the soul is drawn into the body with a staggering motion."[19] This is humorously touched on when Primrose, in the storm, "comes staggering in every so often to reassure me". Lowry is at times over-ingenious in the use of his myth. He represents his Martin as "heroically" reading "a few pages of William Empson's *Seven Types of Ambiguity* each night before going to sleep, just to keep his hand in, as it were, and to keep up with the times. . . ." So he is capable of representing the "defiling" or staining of the bodily vesture of the soul, and its consequent anguish, in the following terms:

> Crash! Coffee, milk, etc. falls into Primrose's lap and on the floor. I fear she will be scalded (she was too) but she is wailing because her pretty new red corduroy slacks are stained.

The sleep into which Psyche falls in the myth is interpreted by Taylor as representing the Platonic sleep of the soul, which, if not made vigilant and alert by the intellect, will "descend to Hades, and be overwhelmed with a sleep perfectly profound."[20]

> The death of the soul is, while merged, or baptized, as it were, in the present body, to descend into matter, and be filled with impurity . . . For to be plunged into matter is to descend into Hades, and fall asleep.[21]

This helps to explain the insistent use of "Frère Jacques", repeated *seven times* in the story, which moreover both begins and ends with this song. What it asks is "Brother, are you asleep?" It also calls for the ringing of the matin bells (of spiritual awakening); and it announces in turn both doom and salvation. It may therefore be taken that one of the major themes of the story is the importance of intellect in rousing the soul from its lethargy and fear. The tradition within which

Lowry was working was centrally intellectualist; the soul, or affective principle in man, was saved not by love alone, but by love under the guidance of intellect, the divine principle in man. In spite of its fearful voyage, the S.S. *Diderot* is travelling eastward to the realm of light and of the gods, and it bears a name that does homage to the enlightenment of the mind.

The story ends with the awakening of the passengers to arrival at the harbour, signalled as in "The Ancient Mariner" by the lighthouse ("Bishop light") and with the engines ringing the matins of a new dawn ("Sonnez les matines!"). That this is the dawn of love is made plain by the gloss from Coleridge:

> And to teach by his own example, love and reverence to all things that God made and loveth.

Finally, lest it be thought that Lowry unfairly left his readers without a warning of the kind of attention he was hoping for, we must note a hint given early in the story:

> Brilliant comment of a person to whom I once lent *Ulysses* on returning it the next day: "Thanks awfully. Very good." (Lawrence also said: "The whole is a strange assembly of apparently incongruous parts, slipping past one another.")

This is a clear enough warning to the reader not to suppose that "Through the Panama" is itself a "strange assembly of apparently incongruous parts", a series of heavily annotated travel notes, and nothing more. Lowry, it seemed, hoped that he would find readers who would have more to say about his story than: "Thanks awfully. Very good." The choice of *Ulysses* as an illustration of philistine inattentiveness is perhaps not as helpful as it was intended to be; one of the problems for an esoteric writer is to judge with any accuracy what degree of knowledge he may expect his readers to supply. It does however suggest that the use made of the sea-voyage is not simply derived from "The Ancient Mariner", but that Lowry recognized, or thought he recognized, the presence of the Ulysses myth in Coleridge's poem.

"Through the Panama" is scarcely so successful a story as others in this volume in which myth and reality are more subtly mixed. Its interest lies in the open exposure of the method, and of its relationship to classical eschatology; and this in turn suggests that we might do well to turn to "The Ancient Mariner" once again, with the help of Lowry's insights into that poem and into its relationship to the tradition.

If there is indeed a deliberate use of the neo-Platonic tradition in this story, it seems fruitless to ask where Lowry might have come across it. Interest in neo-

Platonism and the publishing of Taylor's works flourished in America until 1890, as Professor Harper records.²² It is possible that Lowry came across Taylor either directly or through conversation in the course of his research into the esoteric. During the past eighty years the tradition has almost entirely vanished from sight. Those of us with a predominantly academic education are only now beginning to realize its earlier importance; but an adventurous and voracious reader, seeking for what might feed rather than deaden the imagination, might well, like Yeats, have turned to the neo-Platonic tradition as a source of new significance and vitality.

(1970)

FOOTNOTES

1 Perle Epstein, *The Private Labyrinth of Malcolm Lowry — Under the Volcano and the Cabbala*, New York, 1969.
2 Kathleen Raine and George Mills Harper, *Thomas Taylor the Platonist*, Princeton, 1969. (Referred to hereafter as *Taylor*.)
3 Malcolm Lowry, *Hear Us O Lord From Heaven Thy Dwelling Place*, Philadelphia and New York, 1961.
4 "Ulyxem existimamus esse intellectum animae ducem; socios, mentis agitationes et congenitas vires atque facultates." *De Ulixis Erroribus ethice explicatae,* tr. Johannes Columbus, Stockholm, 1678, p. 23.
5 "But our true country, like that of Ulysses, is from whence we came, and where our father lives." Plotinus, *On the Beautiful,* quoted in Thomas Taylor, *Porphyrius, Select Works,* London, 1823, p. 271.
6 Thomas Taylor, *The Philosophical and Mathematical Commentaries of Proclus,* 2 vols., London, 1792, II, p. 287. (Hereafter referred to as *Proclus.*)
7 *Proclus,* II, p. 294.
8 *Proclus,* II, p. 289.
9 *Proclus,* II, p. 292.
10 Franz Cumont, *Astrology and Religion among the Greeks and Romans,* tr. J. B. Baker, London, 1912, p. 105. See also Dupuis, *Origines de tous les Cultes,* 10 vols., Paris, 1834, VI, p. 108.
11 *Proclus,* II, p. 289.
12 *Taylor,* pp. 313-4.
13 Cicero, *Disputations,* I, xix, 43, in *Tusculan Disputations,* ed. J. E. King, London, 1927.
14 *Taylor,* p. 156 (from Porphyry.)
15 Thomas Taylor, *The Fable of Cupid and Psyche,* London, 1795, p. ix.
16 *Cupid and Psyche,* p. vi.
17 *Cupid and Psyche,* p. vi.
18 *Cupid and Psyche,* p. vii.
19 *Cupid and Psyche,* pp. viii - ix.
20 *Cupid and Psyche,* p. xiv.
21 *Cupid and Psyche,* p. xv.
22 *Taylor,* pp. 49-102.

LOWRY'S PURGATORY

Versions of "Lunar Caustic"

David Benham

IN 1934 MALCOLM LOWRY spent a few days in New York's Bellevue Mental Hospital. Horrified by what he saw there, he wrote a story, now lost, about a journalist, who, through a misunderstanding is detained at the hospital. Two years later Lowry recast the story as a novella, called *The Last Address*; and in 1940 he produced yet another version, titled *Swinging the Maelstrom*. At his death he was working on a melding of these two versions, to be called *Lunar Caustic*. Lowry himself was not to complete the melding,[1] but typescripts of the two versions are extant; we find in them not two successive states of a single work so much as two distinct works which differ considerably in method and intention.

In Lowry's original conception of *The Voyage That Never Ends* as "a Dantesque trilogy," *Lunar Caustic* was to play the Purgatorio to *Under the Volcano*'s Inferno. This provides a useful hint, because Purgatory is a kind of median between Heaven and Hell, a place of transition where opposites meet. Here evil is cauterized from the soul — lunar caustic itself is the painful but medically effective silver nitrate — and knowing this, the soul is ecstatic in its agony; and, although the process is a kind of death, this death is the prelude to rebirth. But modern man cannot commit himself to such a Dantesque conception of Purgatory, even as a metaphor; his faith in salvation is not strong enough. The hospital's patients, like Purgatory's sinners, are allowed no rest; but the patients' painful shuffling around the ward is no more than a mindless "marathon of the dead." The world of *Lunar Caustic* is deeply ambiguous, and is closer to hell than to heaven.

Ambiguity runs through the descriptions both of New York and the hospital itself. The city we see in the story is one in which the transitory is most in evidence. Its factories wave a farewell to life; the ships which come and go bring sometimes a suggestion of hope, but more often of hopelessness. The cry of the hospital patients is described as

> ... partly a cheer and partly a wailing shriek, like some cry of the imprisoned spirit of New York itself, that spirit haunting the abyss between Europe and America and which broods like futurity over the Western Ocean.

Encompassing the polarity between joy and despair, placed uneasily between the New World and the Old, New York personifies a kind of insecurity. It is a city perched on the edge of a chasm.

The hospital, which is at once a prison and an asylum, lies on the East River in the centre of this city of shifting meanings. In the two wharves before the observation ward, we are presented again with the juxtaposition of life and death, of hope and despair; on the one is the powerhouse and the hanging noose, while moored at the other are the white and blue boats "which seemed to tell as they nudged and nibbled ceaselessly at the suicidal blackness of the water, of white and blue girls in summer." Between the wharves is the wrecked barge on which, momentarily, the protagonist sees the crumpled body of a sailor; this barge, to which the boy Garry will return again and again in his stories, is the external emblem of the world of decay in which the patients live. Throughout the description of the setting, opposites coexist, but the negative elements predominate; we are made more aware of death than of life, of decay more than of any possible regeneration.

The ambivalence of the outside world is reflected in the patients and staff of the hospital. Garry, for example, is an entertaining innocent, but one who has committed a horrible crime. He is a moral paradox personified; neither guilty nor guiltless, in him the cycle of innocence — guilt — repentance — redemption is broken. He is creative, but this creativity can be seen both as an attempt to formulate a vision of reality and as an attempt to avoid coming to terms with reality. Again, we can see in Claggart a conscientious doctor who is doing his best in an almost impossible situation, and an insensitive bully who cares little for his patients.

In this world where orientation is impossible, Sigbjørn Lawhill, the protagonist of *The Last Address*, is utterly alone; his father and his son are dead, his wife has left him. As a sailor, he is related to no particular place. There is nothing, either in terms of awareness of the past or relationships in the present, by which his personality might be defined; he is a man in a vacuum, a man without

57

identity. *The Last Address* is an account of his attempt to find himself in relation to others; for only by caring for and helping others can he escape the limitations of his own mind. This theme is adumbrated to his cryptic shout as he enters the hospital:

> *"Veut-on que je disparaisse, que je plonge, à la recherche de l'anneau . . .* I am sent to save my father, to find my son, to heal the eternal horror of three, to resolve the immedicable horror of opposites."

Yet Lawhill is attracted by the isolation he has to escape from; like Geoffrey Firmin, he is drawn to extinguish the self in alcoholic oblivion. The dichotomy within his own mind parallels those in the outside world.

The only way Lawhill can structure his world at the beginning of the story is through his "hysterical identification" with Melville; he integrates his experiences in the hospital by relating them to the patterns of experience which Melville works out in *Moby Dick* and *Billy Budd*. He associates, for example, the boy Garry with Melville's Pip, who, by losing his sanity, saw into a deeper reality; and while watching the groping hand during the puppet-show, he murmurs to himself "Leviathan." The identification with Melville not only serves as an indication of Lawhill's neurotic perception of the world, but also forms a major structural element in the story. Lawhill is associated both with the doomed Pequod and the alienated Ahab; the first quotation from *Moby Dick* which is applied to him suggests some impending disaster — "feeling that he encompassed in his stare oceans from which might be revealed that phantom destroyer of himself." Like Ahab, he has to risk destruction in order to test reality, and the destruction might be total annihilation — insanity or some irrevocable psychic death — or the necessary prelude to regeneration.

The first people Lawhill sees on waking up in the hospital are Garry and Horowitz, the spiritual father and son for whom he has been searching. They are ostensibly in the hospital because their insanity is dangerous — Garry has killed a young girl and Horowitz has threatened to kill his brother-in-law's family; nevertheless Lawhill cannot accept that they are, in any significant sense of the word, insane. He feels that Garry is a kind of unlettered Rimbaud, a boy whose obsession with the decay which permeates the world reveals a perceptive intuition which is fundamentally artistic; the stories which Claggart dismisses as normally abnormal fantasies are, to Lawhill, frightening and valid visions of chaos. Similarly, he sees Horowitz as the Wandering Jew, a man who epitomizes in himself suffering mankind, and is sympathetic to his claim that he has been institutionalized because of his Communist views.

With the companionship of these two people, Lawhill begins to take an interest in those around him. He is quickly sickened by the degradation and casual cruelty which seem an accepted part of the hospital life, and, realizing his own relative health, comes to feel that he has a responsibility to draw attention to the patients' situation. Yet at the same time, in watching the derelicts trapped in the hospital, he becomes increasingly aware of the ambiguities of existence; when he sees the old men eating, he "gradually thought he understood the meaning of death, not as a sudden dispatch of violence, but as a function of life." There can be no unity within life itself, for the unity is composed of both life and death; terror is inescapable. Opposites collapse into one another: "even Nature herself is shot through with jitteriness."

For Lawhill, insanity is often an understandable response to an insane world; the job of the physician is not to teach his patients to adapt to this world, but to give them a new awareness of themselves. With his new-found concern for others, he tries to explain to Claggart that many of the patients are being brought to a debased and servile acceptance of themselves and of the world. "Many", he argues, "who are supposed to be mad here . . . are simply people who perhaps once saw, however confusedly, the necessity for change in themselves, for *rebirth*." But Claggart, while admitting that the hospital is less than perfect, has no difficulty in discrediting Lawhill's central arguments. He sees Lawhill's complaints about the inhumanity of the hospital as merely reflecting his refusal to accept authority, and his perception of the patients' need for rebirth as no more than a projection of his own neurosis. He never admits that Lawhill's ideas have any kind of objectivity; they arise only from "his own state". When apparently talking about other patients, he is really talking about himself; in describing Garry as an unformed Rimbaud, he is merely playing out his own desire to write.

In this clash between Lawhill and Claggart, it is difficult to say that either is right or wrong. While Claggart's name, the parallels with Melville,[2] and the extreme distrust which leads the doctor to dismiss *Billy Budd* itself as a fabrication on Lawhill's part all suggest that truth, or at least goodness, lies with Lawhill in the shifting ambiguities set up in the episode, both are, in their own terms, men of goodwill. They simply cannot communicate; there is no way for Lawhill to express his ideas within Claggart's terms of reference, and therefore he cannot persuade him to change the situation. Under this trial he begins to validate Claggart's analysis; he is reduced to bitter and insulting sarcasm, to fantasizing on his experience, and to challenging the doctor to a test of strength.

The ENCOUNTER WITH Claggart represents the farthest extension of Lawhill's attempt to live in the outside world and to help those around him, and with his failure he begins to slide back into the abyss of his own self-absorption. Looking out at the city from the annexe to Claggart's office, he sees that a storm is gathering; symbolically it is the storm which threatens to engulf humanity as well as his own mind, but only the patients in the hospital, rejected by the "sane" world, are aware of its approach. As the storm breaks Lawhill feels for a moment a sense of release, of "being already outside, free to run with the wind if he wished." But the hope that regeneration will come with the storm is raised only to be immediately extinguished, for he realizes that the bars on the windows are only the external counterparts of the spiritual bars which are fixed in his own mind. This recognition of the fundamental identity between the inner world and outer is, for Lawhill, the last twist of the knife; he is trapped not merely in the hospital or in the world, but within his own psyche, and he is himself a product of the decay which he finds at the centre of the world. Man's state is hopeless; unable to reach outside himself, he can never become complete. In despair, Lawhill sums up the immense agony of the story in a passage which draws together the East River, the grotesque ships which pass on it, and the equally grotesque minds which brood over it:

> This world of the river was one where everything was uncompleted while functioning in degeneration, from which as from Garry's barge, the image of their own shattered or unformed souls was cast back at them. Yes, it was as if all complementary factors had been withdrawn from this world! Its half-darkness quivered with the anguish of separation from the real light; just as in his nightmare, the tortoise crawled in agony looking for its shell, and nails hammered held nothing together, or one-winged birds dropped exhausted across a maniacal, sunless moon.

The forces working to destroy Lawhill begin to close in. The appearance of the *Martha's Vineyard* reminds him of the trip he took with his wife to New Bedford — the place from which Melville started his whaling voyage; and he begins to see a recurring pattern emerging in the chaos of the storm. His own quest for truth or destruction began at the same place as Melville's; and now, in the hospital, he is within sight of "the last address" at which Melville finished *Moby Dick*. Lawhill remembers that the ship which had brought him to New Bedford was, appropriately, the *Providence*; and this ship, at the height of the storm, sails past the hospital. Yet though the name of this ship, and its reappearance at this crucial moment, reinforce the idea that a pattern underlies the world's chaos, the pattern remains one of anguish. The patients, seeing the *Provi-*

dence pass, rush to the window and begin to scream, and their scream is associated with the "mechanic calamity of the rocking city".

Lawhill learns that his friendship with Garry is to be broken; he is returned to the isolation in which he began. At this moment a seaplane appears — as a roar associated with a seaplane had accompanied the groping, menacing white hand during the puppet-show — which becomes, in a terrifying fantasy, the Moby Dick which is to destroy him. The destruction comes in a flash of lightning, but it proves to be neither total extinction nor the shattering of the old self which is the necessary prelude to rebirth; instead he suffers a spiritual annihilation which presages his physical death. As Garry tells Claggart, "It only looks like spring." The regeneration which Lawhill had hoped for cannot come about; in the world in which he finds himself he is condemned to the life-in-death of perpetual incompleteness.

He is little changed by his stay in the hospital. When he leaves he immediately starts to drink again; and he still searches for human contact, imagining passersby to be his relatives, or patients he had met in the hospital. As he throws his empty bottle at an obscene sketch on a lavatory wall which symbolizes for him all the obscenity in the world at large, he remembers how Garry had described the murder of the girl: "It was only a little scratch." The two acts of violence link Lawhill and Garry together, and he is forced to recognize the paradoxical duality of human nature — the coexistence of innocence with guilt, of compassion with a frightening capacity for violence — as operating within himself. Man's nature is such that he is inevitably condemned to suffer; and if patterns underlie chaos, the patterns themselves have no meaning and imply no value. Lawhill's only escape lies in embracing his isolation. At the end of the story he returns to the presexual state which Garry had never felt, finding security and oblivion in retiring "to the obscurest corner of the bar, where, curled up like an embryo . . . Sigbjørn Lawhill could not be seen at all."

The Last Address is an often terrifying account of a man trying to raise himself out of the pit of self-absorption, but it is a work which leaves the reader dissatisfied. One of the reasons, I think, is that the onus of blame for Lawhill's failure is placed largely on the world outside him. His rejection by a man as unsympathetic as Claggart constitutes an evasion of a central problem — the extent to which Lawhill is able to bring himself to accept responsibility for others. Consequently the questions we want to ask — to what extent he has chosen isolation in the past, and to what extent he is continuing to choose it in the present — can never be answered. And because we cannot determine the validity of his observations of the world around him, we can attach no value to his final non-solution.

Swinging the Maelstrom is a reworking of the situation and setting of *The Last Address*, but two crucial changes — the protagonist's failure as a jazz musician, and his relationship with the doctor — lead toward a resolution of these problems. Bill Plantagenet's failure as a musician is used in part to emphasize the fact that his isolation is the product of an inadequacy in himself; it is both a symptom of and a metaphor for his total spiritual failure. This point is made when he tries to persuade Philip, the doctor, that he is not a good piano player because his hands cannot stretch an octave. Philip replies, apparently irrelevantly, "You didn't leave Ruth because your hands couldn't stretch an octave," but he later adds, "Perhaps it was your heart you couldn't make stretch an octave."

The fact that Bill and Philip are cousins gives Bill a position of responsibility among the patients. As he develops a friendship with the boy and the old man (who is called Kalowsky in this version), he comes to feel, like Lawhill, that the hospital cannot help them. He determines to discuss their cases with Philip, and they accept him as a potential saviour. But Bill's job is harder than Lawhill's, for his cousin, unlike Claggart, is a humane and perceptive man. Philip works as well as he can in a situation which he cannot entirely control; during the puppet-show it seems to Bill that the drama

> ... was being diverted from its course by some sinister disposition of the puppeteer's; he sensed ... the doctor's increasing discomfort, as of a god, he thought, who discovers all over again that man is not long to be trusted with the strings of his destiny.

However, the most striking aspect of Philip's character, as contrasted with Claggart's, is his experience of horror. When Bill begins to suggest that the doctor does not understand suffering, Philip reveals a knowledge far deeper than his own; deeper because, while Bill has inflicted suffering on himself, Philip has to live with the responsibility of inflicting it on others.

In their relationship as cousins, their detachment from the patients, their joint responsibility for Garry and Kalowsky, and their knowledge of horror, Philip and Bill form a two-man community within the hospital. Despite the slight ambiguity in their relationship, marked by the "certain rebelliousness" which Philip rouses in Bill, and the long silences which occasionally punctuate their conversations, they can like and understand one another. Nevertheless, Philip is the greater person; his knowledge is wider, his insight, suffering, and humanity deeper. As a result, Bill finds himself unable to press his arguments for Garry and Kalowsky;

instead he comes to accept the necessity for the apparently inhuman institution of which Philip is a part. Lawhill failed in his plea to Claggart because they could not communicate; Bill fails precisely because he can sympathize with Philip's point of view so readily.

In becoming, in effect, part of the system which is crushing the patients, Bill fails to live up to the spirit of his promise to Garry and Kalowsky He is unable to tell them that he has implicitly condoned their treatment in the hospital, and so for the first time a false note enters into their friendship; he says little to them on returning from Philip's office, and refuses to meet Garry's eyes. As a result of his community with his cousin, he is driven to isolate himself once more. This isolation, however, is not quite what Lawhill reverts to at the end of *The Last Address*, for while Lawhill has looked at the world and decided, in effect, that nothing could be done, Bill realizes the necessity of doing something; his guilty participation in the system which has produced Garry forces him to recognize his responsibility to combat the evil around him. His phone call to a relative of one of the patients suggests his need to cast himself, in some sense, in the role of a doctor.

His release comes after he has momentarily actualized the violence within himself by throwing his bottle at the obscene sketch. In conversation with a friendly stranger, to whom he introduces himself as "Herman Melville", he mistakes the name of a passing ship; the name he hears is the *Acushnet* — the ship on which Melville made his whaling voyage. The ship turns out to be a Spanish Loyalist, engaged in conflict with the White Whale of Fascism, and although there is danger in joining her, she offers an escape from the paralyzed self-absorption which is Lawhill's only response to a world of irresolvable ambiguity. Bill is able to accept the implication that he, like Melville, must voyage, must be prepared to risk total annihilation. He is still isolated, since he has lost contact with Philip, Garry, and Kalowsky, but he has broken out of the self-destructive circuit which had trapped Lawhill, and is ready to renew his spiritual quest.

A s STUDIES IN ALIENATION, *The Last Address* and *Swinging the Maelstrom* are less compelling than Lowry's major works; they reveal neither the appalling insight into man's potential for self-destruction which we find in *Under the Volcano* and the later Mexican novels, nor the awareness of man's need to relate himself to his total environment which is a central theme in *Hear Us O Lord From Heaven Thy Dwelling Place*. But though imperfect, they are deeply moving, and they enable us to draw some tentative conclusions about *The Voyage That Never Ends*, which was to have been composed, as Lowry first conceived it, of the trilogy: *Under the Volcano*; *Lunar Caustic*; *In Ballast to the White Sea*.

The basic pattern of the trilogy was, as Lowry called it, "withdrawal and return". The withdrawal is from the community of mankind into a kind of hell — the hell of alcoholism, of utter isolation, of self-absorption; and this self-absorption is also self-abnegation, a complete loss of the individual sense of identity. This descent into hell is an integral part of the process of regeneration, a recognition of the powers of darkness which operate in the human psyche; but it must be followed by a re-entry into the world. The protagonist begins to relate to and identify with others, and with this identification comes the realization that he has to act. The final step is his complete involvement in the world; with action, his human potentialities, his ability to love and to create, become actual.

In *Under the Volcano*, Geoffrey Firmin has gone so far in his self-absorption that he cannot make the re-entry. We learn from the letter which Laruelle reads in the first chapter the desperation with which the Consul yearns for Yvonne's return, but when she actually appears he is utterly incapable of responding to her, either verbally or sexually. As the day wears on, he is drawn increasingly to Parian and the Farolito; when, with the discovery of the dying peasant, he is faced with the human necessity for action, he is not even tempted to play the Good Samaritan. Finally he chooses his isolation. "I love hell," he tells Hugh and Yvonne; "I can't wait to get back there." Yet in fact he has no choice, for, like Milton's Satan, he has become his own hell; his self-absorption has been carried to such an extent that his entire spiritual energy is channeled towards his own destruction.

The Last Address is an account of an attempt to make the return, but the attempt fails because the only relationships which the protagonist can enter into cannot, by their nature, survive. Bill Plantagenet, on the other hand, motivated by his kinship with his cousin and his sense of guilt toward Garry, is ultimately able to act; he begins at last to orient himself in the outside world.

Lowry's account of *In Ballast to the White Sea* (in a letter to David Markson dated August 25, 1951) indicates that the novel reworked and extended the themes of *Lunar Caustic*. The protagonist (called A in the letter), like Lawhill and Plantagenet, is trapped in a circuit of inaction; he drinks heavily, is unable to relate in any significant way to others, and can only identify with a writer, X, who is personally unknown to him. A's identification with X does not serve to structure reality for him; it is so strong that it becomes a threat to his own identity. Obsessed by the idea that he has in some sense been written by X, A is paralyzed by his inability to find any source of value in the world.

Like Plantagenet, he is eventually able to break out of his inaction; after a period of hesitation he undertakes his voyage to the ambiguous White Sea, with the intention of trying to find X. The journey also turns into a pilgrimage to the past, for A, after being paid off from his ship, finds himself close to his mother's grave. In the churchyard he meets a girl with whom he falls in love — the setting clearly indicates the idea of rebirth — and in doing so he re-establishes contact with others. Finally the series of coincidences which leads him to X, and the correspondences between them, suggest some design in the chaos which both perceive; and this experience renews each man's faith in his creativity. The search for value is over; it is found to lie not in the individual self, but in fulfilling the self through interaction with others.

(1970)

FOOTNOTES

[1] An edition of *Lunar Caustic* by Earle Birney and Margerie Lowry which combines the two earlier versions has been published in *Paris Review* 29, and by Jonathan Cape (London, 1968). Lowry's typescripts are held by the Special Collections Division of the U.B.C. Library, and are catalogued under the title *Lunar Caustic*. The latest complete text of *The Last Address* is ts. 4, while ts. 8 is the best copy of *Swinging the Maelstrom*. My quotations are taken from the Cape edition.

[2] Claggart is the false accuser of *Billy Budd*. The episode parallels Chapter 20 of Melville's novel: in each case the innocent and honest (Billy Budd, Lawhill, and, by extension, Garry) is accused by duplicity (the two Claggarts); the innocent is left literally or figuratively speechless, and can only express himself in violence.

ART AS THE
WRITER'S MIRROR

Literary Solipsism in "Dark as the Grave"

George Woodcock

In the early pages of *Dark as the Grave Wherein My Friend Is Laid*, Sigbjørn Wilderness is standing in a queue in the Los Angeles Airport, waiting with his wife Primrose for a plane to Mexico. His travel excitement, his anxieties and tensions, coalesce to produce an extraordinary feeling of anticipation and of pending enlightenment:

> ... he had suddenly a glimpse of a flowing like an eternal river; he seemed to see how life flowed into art: how life gives art a form and meaning and flows into life, yet life has not stood still; that was what was always forgotten: how life transformed by art sought further meaning through art transformed by life; and now it was as if this flowing, this river, changed, without appearing to change, became a flowing of consciousness, of mind, so that it seemed that for them too, Primrose and he, just beyond that barrier, lay some meaning, or the key to a mystery that would give some meaning to their ways on earth; it was as if he stood on the brink of an illumination, on the near side of something tremendous, which was to be explained beyond, in that midnight darkness ...

Then the loudspeaker — embodying actuality — breaks in on Sigbjørn's thoughts, and his expectations droop as the queue moves forward in a body towards the barrier.

This is one of the crucial passages of *Dark as the Grave*. It illuminates the central action of the book, the seeking back through life to events and episodes that became the substance of a work of art. It also reflects faithfully the mood which *Dark as the Grave* is likely to produce in most readers — that of an expectation never wholly fulfilled, an experience whose incompleteness reflects the provisional character of the book as it is presented to us.

66

At the end of 1945, a few months after the end of the Second World War, Lowry and his second wife, Margerie, set out on a trip to Mexico in which he intended to revisit the places which had provided the setting for *Under the Volcano*; he wanted especially to find a Mexican friend in Oaxaca who had been the original of the drunken Dr. Vigil in that novel. Lowry travelled in a state of great anxiety, since — with a caution which hindsight makes appear extraordinary — the publishers were hesitant about accepting *Under the Volcano*, while the appearance of Charles Jackson's novel of drunkenness, *The Lost Weekend*, seemed a formidable challenge and aroused, in Lowry's intensely paranoiac mind, the fear that he would be accused of plagiarism when his own novel did appear. The journey was punctuated with roaring bouts of tequila and mescal drinking, and on one occasion Lowry slashed his wrists, though clumsily enough for one to assume that his desire to leave this world was at most tentative. The Lowrys visited Cuernavaca and Taxco, travelling like tourists, and eventually reached Oaxaca, to find that the man they were seeking had been dead for years and to return immediately.

Later, looking through his journals of the trip, Lowry exclaimed, "By God, we have a novel here!", and for five years, on and off, he worked on *Dark as the Grave* until, in 1952, he stowed it incomplete into a bank strongbox. There it remained untouched until after his death in 1957. Some time afterwards Margerie Lowry and a young American scholar, Douglas Day, undertook to edit the mass of notes and drafts of which the seven hundred and five page manuscript consisted. They discovered that there were many false starts on paths that led nowhere, many passages that seemed irrelevant to the general text, and some episodes in as many as five different versions. They rightly decided that even the slightest rewriting would be inadmissible on both aesthetic and ethical grounds, and proceeded by extensive and careful cutting to produce a consecutive, unrepetitious and relatively smooth narrative. Since this involved making choices where alternatives existed, and presumably dropping some roughly written passages, they in fact gave their own shape to the book as certainly as if they had set out to change its actual pattern of words. Since they give no indication of any kind where they made their cuts, we cannot judge either the extent or importance of their omissions, and we have therefore no means of speculating on Lowry's true intentions at the time when he abandoned his work on *Dark as the Grave*.

The intent of the editors in following the procedure they have chosen is evident. They wished to present a smoothly running novel that would interest the intelligent general reader. They might have saved themselves the effort, for *Dark*

67

as the Grave — one realizes in the first twenty pages — is likely to be of interest only to Lowry cultists and to literary scholars, and both groups would undoubtedly have preferred the novel in that unsmoothed chaos which would have told us so much more about the writer's mind and his ways of working. No-one who has not read *Under the Volcano* beforehand will be able to follow the innumerable and complex allusions to its episodes and characters which form part of the basic texture of *Dark as the Grave*. Indeed, that work as it now stands exists only in terms of its relationship to the earlier novel. It is barely fiction, since it recounts with hardly any essential change the journey the Lowrys undertook in 1945. Sigbjørn Wilderness *is* Lowry in a far deeper and more literal way than most characters can be described as *being* the novelists who create them, and we shall be a great deal nearer to reality if we drop on the author's behalf the pretence that this is a novel in any true sense, and regard it as a combination of travel narrative, spiritual autobiography and literary history, heightened here and there with exaggeration and a relatively slight measure of invention. *Under the Volcano* is actually renamed; it becomes *The Valley of the Shadow of Death*, but most of its characters appear with their names unchanged, and a good deal of fascinating information is provided on the way Lowry went about constructing it. We learn how the fictional town of Quauhnahuac was created by combining characteristics of Cuernavaca and Oaxaca, and how characters came into being by people remembered from real life dividing like amoebas, so that some of their traits went to make one individual in a novel and the rest to make another. Lowry himself, of course, was the most notable example of this kind of division; much of him went into Hugh Firmin, but far more into Geoffrey, the tragic Consul.

THE DELVING into which one is led inevitably by a reading of *Dark as the Grave* can take one only towards eventual comparison between the two books, a comparison which in its turn involves broader speculations on the imperfections of Lowry's achievement. *Under the Volcano* was a work of extraordinary resourcefulness. It is true that Lowry's limitations were evident even in that book; he could not create a character in depth that did not contain a great deal of himself, and in consequence — though the incidental grotesques who walked on to say a word or two or strike a pose were often striking and amusing — his second-rank characters, like Yvonne and Jacques, were shallowly conceived and executed. But the Consul's inner life, his great drunken soliloquies, his mad transmutations into personal fantasy of the intrusions of the outer world, are splendidly created, and the orchestration with which he unites this subjective landscape with the menacing outer landscape of Mexico itself and with the symbolism of the Day of the Dead is superb, as is the structural power with which all this action, with its vast trailing burdens of the memories of several lives and of numerous literary and metaphysical allusions, is englobed except for the first prologue chapter into the unity of a single day.

Dark as the Grave contains passages of excellent Lowry comedy, mingled with others of embarrassing sentimentality in which the relationship of the travelling couple is portrayed, and at times one becomes as interested in Sigbjørn's wayward thoughts as in the macabre fancies of the Consul. But the architectonic achievements of *Under the Volcano* are absent from the depressingly linear structure of *Dark as the Grave*; the literary and philosophic allusions are far more meagre, and the characters are far less complex and compelling. Transfiguration has not, in other words, taken place. There is too much talk about art, and too little art.

Dark as the Grave does not, in fact, make its own universe, like *Under the Volcano*; it revolves as a satellite. Both works, in Lowry's mind, were intended as parts of the Proustian scheme he had evolved in which all his writings would be united in a great literary continuum. In practice, however, the link between these particular books is not one of equality, but of subordination. It resembles that between Gide's *Les faux monnayeurs* and the *Journal des "faux monnayeurs"* in which Gide reveals how the major work was constructed.

The dependence of *Dark as the Grave* in its turn brings into question the extent to which Lowry was capable of sustaining the level of creation achieved in *Under the Volcano*. It is perhaps significant that *Hear Us O Lord From Heaven Thy Dwelling Place*, and particularly "The Forest Path to the Spring", is very much better in both style and resolution than *Dark as the Grave*. Perhaps the experience of creating *Under the Volcano* was so intense that any other book Lowry might write on Mexico must be robbed of light in its mountainous shadow, while of his notably different experiences in British Columbia he could write freshly and originally. On this point we shall be able to judge finally only when the two remaining incomplete Lowry novels are published. *La Mordida* concerns Mexico; *October Ferry to Gabriola* concerns British Columbia.

The question still remains on one's mind: how in five years — even of intermittent work — and after so many starts and so many drafts, Lowry could leave a work so unformed as *Dark as the Grave*. Much of the detail is excellent: vivid writing, fine observation. But, seen as a whole, the book lacks shape, just as its characters lack individual natures, are mere buds still attached to the parent stem of the author's mind. The reasons are partly personal, embedded in Lowry's insecure and fear-ridden nature. But Lowry's actions were at least partly conditioned by solipsistic attitudes prevalent in modern European literature, which in their turn stem from the nineteenth century romantic cult of the artist. Not merely was the artist's work interesting, as in earlier centuries; the artist himself, anonymous in the past, became even more interesting. To writers the proper study of mankind became the writer, and out of this preoccupation sprang the long line of works centred on the act of artistic creation. Occasionally, like Thomas Mann in *Dr. Faustus*, the writer would choose an artist of another kind, but in such works as Mann's *Death in Venice*, Huxley's *Point Counter Point*, Proust's *À la recherche du temps perdu*, the writer-hero emerges in his full glory, and it is not far from this stage to the point at which the writer-hero becomes lost to the world around him in the contemplation of his own work. Into this circle Gide came with that extraordinary piece of mirror-work, *Les faux monnayeurs*, in which the writer-hero is writing a work identical with that which contains him, and Lowry follows with *Dark as the Grave*, in which he assumes that his process of literary creation will be as interesting to the reader as the created work itself.

It is significant that, in both these cases, the most solipsistic work of the author in question is the least successful. "Life transformed by art" does not in fact seek "further meaning through art transformed by life." Once created, the work of art is its own world, but into its creation life must enter. Art made out of art is always sterile, as the downward path of painting in the last twenty years has shown. The author walks a difficult path; to be truly successful, he must learn, as Lowry did in *Under the Volcano*, to orchestrate the world within him and the world without; only out of such a combination emerges the transcending symphony of art achieved. The dangerous point is that which Lowry later reached, when the process of art becomes so completely fascinating, so all-absorbing, that life outside the artist's mind loses its meaning and its immediacy, and the completion of the work ceases to be important because the work is a projection of the artist's life and cannot come to a close until that is ended. Literary solipsism, like any other form of artistic solipsism, is in the end regressive, and involves the surrender of past achievements.

(1969)

THE WRITER AS CONSCIOUSNESS

A View of "October Ferry to Gabriola"

Matthew Corrigan

THERE IS LITTLE EVIDENCE that Lowry could have turned the unfinished manuscript of *October Ferry to Gabriola* into as fine a novel as *Under the Volcano*. Lowry was simply not of a mind to finish things the last ten years of his life. There is not the same urgency in *Gabriola* as in the great novel. *Volcano*'s faults are justified by the character's propulsion toward self-destruction, a propulsion that will probably read to a later age as clearly as Ahab's does to our own, despite some of the same kinds of language excess. We never doubt the seriousness of Geoffrey Firmin's katabasis. *Gabriola* has the same seriousness but the action is missing to anneal the whole, the action-toward-death. *Gabriola* represents the volcanic state of mind drawn out to a fine tremor of existence: given the option of joy over the earlier novel's imperative of despair. We know Dante's paradise is duller than his inferno and we know why it has to be so. Religion and art do not overlap without some loss of nerve. This is not to say that *Gabriola* doesn't work. It does work but it works as something different from what it pretends to be.

Because he laboured on it painstakingly for the last ten years of his life, *Gabriola* manages to survey beautifully that period of Lowry's creativity, a period that represents in many ways his conversion back to life. If there are any doubts after reading the letters and short stories that it was a fertile period, *Gabriola* puts these to rest. As a piece of writing it achieves moments of lyric and philosophic grace that equal anything written in the twentieth century; moments that spring from such a quietness of spirit (a *quietus*, even) that it is difficult to peruse them in the context of a work that describes itself on the surface as a novel.

The infernal and paradisiacal (Eridanus) poles that divided and ruled Lowry's thinking are felt once again, though the pull is positive throughout, inclining finally toward a synthesis of salvation, even of grace. The theme is dispossession, eviction. Ethan and Jacqueline Llewelyn are under edict of eviction from their squatter's shack at Eridanus, on the north shore of Burrard Inlet, opposite Vancouver. They have shared two years of extraordinary, primitive joy: a joy based on the near totality of their rebellion against a polluted, plastic age (the year is 1949); based on a simple return to nature and a learning to love the elements of that nature; but based also on an Ockham balance achieved between reality and fear, of which fear Llewelyn has the usual Lowry inheritance.

> For the first time they had both acquired, though they didn't know it then, a complete faith in their environment, without that environment ever seeming too secure. This was a gift of grace, finally a damnation, and a paradox in itself all at once: for it didn't need to seem secure for them to have faith in its security. Or the little house itself didn't need to. The very immediacy of the eternities by which they were surrounded and nursed; antiquity of mountains, forest, and sea, conspired on every hand to reassure and protect them, as with the qualities of their own seeming permanence . . . Eridanus *was*.

Essentially the novel takes place in Llewelyn's consciousness, though of such a symbiotic and cosmic nature is that consciousness that it tends to become whatever it considers or momentarily takes cognizance of. The book is this consciousness in the state of becoming. Present action takes place on a bus from Victoria to Nanaimo, where the Llewelyns board a ferry for Gabriola Island. They have heard of a sea-captain's house for sale on the island and they are journeying to inspect it. Should the house be unsuitable there is a tract of land they can buy running down to the sea, and Llewelyn is prepared, as before, to build a house with his own hands. Present experiences tend to be few and far between — an incident in a Nanaimo tavern, something seen from the window of a bus — experiences which propel Llewelyn back into his past. The trip is laced with minute correspondences which secure the past in a state of webbed terror. Most of the time we are delving so deeply into the past that its own past becomes significant. The past within the past is explored in depth, so that everything gives way to and becomes part of everything else: a single continuum of consciousness in which time is technically suspended.

The ferry is actually taken but returns because of a sick passenger. The whole trip (Eridanus: Vancouver: Victoria: Nanaimo) seems to enact a geographic flirtation with Eridanus, as though something in the elements refused to let them travel far from home; at several junctures they find themselves pointed homeward, the significance of which does not escape Llewelyn. The book ends with the travellers once again ferrying across the strait to Gabriola. Instead of taking us to the island, however, Lowry lets Llewelyn envision their new life there, a vision very close structurally to the one at the end of *Volcano*, where Firmin imagines a similar Canadian paradise. This sudden projection forward optimistically at the end presages an escape for the Llewelyns from the past that has terrorized them. At least this seems to be Lowry's intention. When the ferry returns to discharge its sick passenger the evening newspapers are taken on board. As the ferry approaches Gabriola they read that city council has reprieved the squatters at Eridanus. They are free to return from exile. Since they are already on their way, the prospect of a more permanent home on the island takes on a new significance. It is as though they have eased clear of their own doom, have escaped the punishment that has been threatening throughout. Salvation is felt as a moment of release that comes when least expected in the throes of an ordeal; it is something to remain humble about, for it retains as its present heritage the remembrance of what it is like to suffer in exile. Such is the Lowry synthesis. We glimpse it partially in "Forest Path to the Spring" and in *Dark as the Grave*; in *Gabriola* it is given its longest moment. What is amazing is that it thrusts through the unfinished manuscript with the clarity and consonance of a single state of mind, suggesting that all of Lowry's later work was reaching toward this conclusion. Surprisingly, his plan for a continuum of works scanning the upsweep of the *Divine Comedy* becomes a reality with this book.

That Ethan Llewelyn is a forty-year-old retired criminal lawyer is almost irrelevant to the book. Why he has given up his Toronto law practice to settle in a west coast shack is never explained. The book in fact is about Lowry's life at Dollarton, British Columbia: his struggle with actual and spiritual eviction, with alcohol, with guilt, with God. At times Lowry manages to objectify his ordeal, to disguise it in the fear or thought of an Ethan Llewelyn, as when Llewelyn is riddled with guilt about not defending a fifteen-year-old boy sentenced to be hanged, a cowardice he connects with an earlier incident at university when he failed to prevent a young friend from hanging himself. Llewelyn is every bit as infirm as Geoffrey Firmin, with occasionally some of the same insight into the mystery of that infirmity. What is most unfinished in this book concerns Llewelyn the lawyer and the reasons for his retreat. Lowry's working notes indicate some of the things he intended to add to facilitate our believing in his character on objective as well as personal grounds. Evidently, we were to be shown how Llewelyn had defended a man he believed innocent, only to learn he was a murderer. Thus his disillusionment and his retreat from civilization. That the book works as well as it does despite its factual imperfections and its structural imbalance indicates, I think, the degree to which Lowry was no mean characterizer, and no ordinary novelist. Finally, it doesn't matter who Llewelyn is trying to be; he is the Lowry persona — he could be no other. The book is the mind of the author at work phenomenologically on the raw substance of experience, narrowed as that experience was through his choice of life-style, through his consciously cultivating one species of suffering, through his latent Manicheism.

Llewelyn's external world makes a bizarre kind of sense. It is constantly telling him something about himself, pumping him with information to help overthrow the fear that the world has gone mad. There are few inert or isolated facts. Films that Llewelyn sees become more real than life itself. He becomes the "Wandering Jew" in a film of that title. He suffers that becoming. Nothing exists for him without prehension, without intentionality. The mountains spining British Columbia are one geologically with the infernal Ixtaccihuatl and Popocatapetl of *Volcano*. In his drunkenness Llewelyn is capable of merging consciousness with Noah, Swedenborg, Edgar Allan Poe, Geoffrey Firmin, and others. The ghost of Poe is omnipresent throughout. Llewelyn looks like Poe physically (to say nothing of the spiritual resemblance). As a student he attended Poe's alma mater. The day of his bus trip, aside from its being the day on which his student friend hanged himself twenty years before, is the hundredth anniversary of Poe's death.

Everything is connected with everything for those with pure vision. The men's section of a bar in Nanaimo (which has "an ugliness the world had not thought of before") seems to take on the "perfect outward expression of his own inner soul, of what it meant, of what it did, even of what awful things could happen in it." Words overheard are "addressed mysteriously to Ethan himself; and moreover . . . every phrase [has] another meaning, perhaps many meanings, intended for his ears alone." Llewelyn has been introduced to the Cabbala by Jacqueline's father, a "white magician" with sundry occult powers, and that too gets drawn into the overall flow of consciousness.

> In fact he could sum up no better their life on the beach than to say it had been, in a manner, *his* cabbala, in the sense that, if he was not mistaken, that system might be regarded on one plane as a means less of accumulating than of divesting oneself — by arrangement, balancing them against their opposites — of unbalanced

ideas: the mind, finally transcending both aspects, regains its lost equilibrium, or for the first time truly discovered it; not unlike, Ethan sometimes supposed, the modern process of psychoanalysis.

When things are going well there is this perfect symbiosis between man and environment, between self and God. Their shack, unlike their other two houses (both of which burned to the ground mysteriously), means more than the usual abode: "they wear it like a shell," they "love it like a sentient being." Eridanus exemplifies a religious wholeness; and love is the cement that secures it fast. Eviction, or its threat, is thus taken as symptomatic of some overlooked and unconfessed evil. Llewelyn has no difficulty screening his past for the appropriate evidence. He sees himself responsible for his friend's suicide; he sees himself a failure as a lawyer who might plead eloquently for the abolition of capital punishment, and for the life of a boy murderer. There is even the fear that he has become too possessive for Eridanus. Guilt is never that simple or unilateral, however. Llewelyn has the added torment of terrible visions — visions of chaos and not of some principle of good controlling the reeling world. His greatest despair comes when under the influence of alcohol.

Significantly, Llewelyn cannot avoid peering into such depths. He needs a sense of hell in his life almost in order to keep his joy sensibly bound. Once he envisions this hell it is enough. An inverse spirit resembling hope begins to point him in the opposite direction and he sees with cleared vision.

> What was important was that he was now convinced there must be some complete triumphant counterpart, hitherto based on hearsay or taken on trust, of that experience he had had, or almost had: as there must be of that abyssal region, some spiritual region maybe of unborn divine thoughts beyond our knowledge . . .
>
> Mightn't he equally well consider that he'd been vouchsafed, was so being vouchsafed, a glimpse into the very workings of creation itself? — indeed with this cognition Ethan seemed to see before his eyes whole universes eternally condensing and re-condensing themselves out of the "immaterial" into the "material", and as the continued visualization of their Creator, being radiated back again. While meantime here on earth the "material" was only cognizable through the mind of man! What was real, what imaginary? Yes, but couldn't the meaning, the message, for *them*, be simply that there *had* been a message at all? Yes, could he not just as well tell himself, as Cyprian of Antioch, that here God had beaten the devil at his own game, that magic was checkmated by miracle! Ethan drank half another beer. Gone was his fright. In its stead was awe. In the beginning was the word. But what unpronounceable Name had visualized the Word?

The only drama is that between present and past consciousness; the only action the will of the moment grappling with a mute past, not so that it can strike out in pure action, but rather so that it can enlarge upon itself, so that it can know itself. The process is self-defeating because of its intoxication, its solipsism. Few prose writers of the modern period have tried (have tormented) the moment of consciousness as Lowry does in this work. What he seems to be emphasizing is the compulsion of modern man to rework past consciousness; suggesting that if man is to constitute himself as a free individual he must first make sense of the nightmare of his past. The posture of Lowry's later work is *retrospective* in this sense. Terror is something experienced when one realizes the significance of the past, when one sees the connection; it does not consist of any present threat. Since all of this ratiocination is intended as a kind of reparation for the future, the present moment tends to be overlooked, if not also to be underlived. There is almost no active present tense in this work.

The fact is Lowry came to think this way as a writer. It represents a dangerously close perspective for a writer to have unless he is a phenomenologist and his subject, quite unabashedly, is the reduction of consciousness. Dangerous because you can't locate the infinite in the general labyrinth of human mind except in terms of a general intentional structure. The result at best is but a frenetic scaffolding that gives the sense of the impending event but never the spectacle itself. The prose takes on the tortured shape of the quest in its circumlocution. The shape of *Gabriola* is that of a vortex out of which something material is about to be hurled. Often nothing is hurled clear; no meaning is adduced and past consciousness is swept into present.

Lowry's is the problem of the poet turned mystic, a problem of learning to face the fact that everything that comes from his creative unconscious is part of everything else in the order of creation, and must be attended to, must be set down in chiselled stone prose, if the final balance is to be maintained. Editing, or what for the average novelist amounts to an ordinary task, is lost sight of in Lowry's later work. Certain parts of *Gabriola* give the feeling that at some later rereading the author would have trimmed or deleted them. Yet the same pieces show us something of the difficulty of doing this for Lowry, because in some way they control parts of the larger whole; they give the feeling of belonging. There is a strange logic behind the excess (the plethora) of this manuscript, a logic akin to that of dreams. It defies ordinary daylight understanding yet demands our attention. I am thinking of the way a person we know reveals himself or herself totally in a dream, becoming through word or deed a full being and doing so in terms that seem totally appropriate to that person; so that on awakening we think,

"Yes, that is exactly what she would say, how she would act." Though nothing of the sort had taken place or would ever take place in real life the dream had effected the imaginative leap that life was too shy or slow to make. The ontological accuracy of the thing strikes us. It is the same with the manuscript of *Gabriola*. Lowry was right, finally, to believe in his continuum of works as he did, to respect the presence of every wandering beggar that passed through his consciousness, lest the indigent turn out to be Christ in disguise. Reading Lowry, if one does it properly, requires more than the usual suspension of disbelief. If the writing works for us, it does so not because it is fiction on its way to becoming a novel, but because it entails a vision of a higher order of creative existence altogether than we ordinarily get in modern literature. It would be difficult to imagine a later age making anything like a fair assessment of our own without such a testament, bleak and solemn as it tends to be.

(1971)

THE LONG VOYAGE HOME

October Ferry to Gabriola

Anthony R. Kilgallin

THE SURE SIGN of a superior writer is that even in his failures he commands respect. Hemingway's *Islands in the Stream* and Lowry's *October Ferry to Gabriola*, hereafter called *Ferry*, both contain solid evidence of literary strength sufficient to win many rounds, but finally inadequate to win again the titles won by earlier works. Posthumous publication of nearly completed works-in-progress is often a damned-if-you-do and damned-if-you-don't affair. However, in the case of these two novels, Mary Hemingway and Margerie Lowry are to be commended far more than chastised. Each widow is adamant that nothing has been added: "I would never try to foist on the public something false. The book was signed by Ernest and it is his and his alone"; "every word must be Malcolm's." Nevertheless, though the right words may or may not be there, one cannot help feeling that the final masterful editing touches are not. Just why each novel, started in the forties, worked on in the fifties and published in the fall of 1970, was left incomplete some time before the tragic death of its writer remains open to conjecture that can never be absolutely ratified. Still, most readers will be in agreement that while these last novels are not their authors' crowning achievements, each contains many passages equal to the best in their masterpieces.

As with all of Lowry's writings, *Ferry* began as a point of departure from a series of factual events. A published letter of fall 1945 to Conrad Aiken told of traumatic encounters with fire while living at Niagara-on-the-Lake, Ontario, where Lowry was completing *Under the Volcano*. (These adventures were transposed into the self-contained short story "The Element Follows You Around, Sir" published in *Show Magazine*, March, 1964, which also serves for chapters 18 to 21 of *Ferry*.) Then, with Margerie, he took a boat from Vancouver to Victoria, a bus from Victoria to Nanaimo and the ferry to Gabriola Island on October 7,

1946 (not 1947 as Lowry tells his editor Albert Erskine in a January, 1954 letter), ninety-eight years to the day after the death of Poe, one of Lowry's kindred spirits. In the same letter to Erskine, on the subject of "The Element Follows You Around Sir," he writes, "Curiously enough I found myself putting the last finishing touches on this bit on Jan. 9, that 1809, was Poe's birthday." (Actually it was January 19, but Lowry's penchant for coincidences probably overlooked this in favour of the fact that Poe was born exactly a century before him, in the same year as another important kindred spirit, Gogol.)

In November, 1950, Lowry wrote his agent, Harold Matson, referring to *Ferry* as "a story which you've had before, but which was no damned good. This we decided we couldn't collaborate on so I have completely rewritten it by myself and finally I'm extremely pleased with it and feel it will be as good as anything I've done, and saleable also." Despite the "finally", *Ferry* was "still a problem child" three years later, and "has cost me more pains than all the *Volcano* put together." At this time Lowry was working also on companion pieces: The stories "Forest Path to the Spring", "Ghostkeeper", and "Present Estate of Pompeii". To Erskine he confided that "where it insists on growing I have to give it its head," even though every extension came only after a slow struggle during which he beseeched everyone from St. Jude, the Saint of the Impossible, to God, to Turgenev, to Poe, to Nordahl Grieg and even to St. Jerome for help.

For, by now, Lowry believed his daemon had "turned what set out to be an innocent and beautiful story of human longing into quite one of the most guilt-laden and in places quite Satanically horrendous documents it has ever been my unfortunate lot to read, let alone have to imagine I wrote." In addition, "it possesses perhaps not one single conventional virtue of the normal story — its character drawing is virtually non-existent, symbols are pointed at blatantly instead of being concealed or subsumed in the material, or better still simply not there at all, it is — or is as it stands — repetitious to the point beyond that which you can believe. It's all done on purpose, and some readers — if they read it once — might have to read it 5 times before they could be convinced anything has happened at all." Unfortunately, the editorial powers at Random House were dissatisfied with a work apparently more in a state of regress than of progress. Lowry was either unaware or had forgotten that the work was to have been ready for publication by November 1, 1953. He thought he had until February 1, 1954, when he expected to have completed a further 140 pages. Faced with a terminated contract against which he had drawn advances, Lowry sent Erskine the self-

79

contained "Element" segment. Whatever momentum *Ferry* did have dissolved in entropy so that, in a letter of May, 1954 to Erskine, Lowry expresses his feeling that "I may consider myself to have stopped the clock at 11.59 P.M. on October 31, 1953." His departure for Europe later that summer, and a mental breakdown in England the following year, during which his doctor forbade him to write on the *Gabriola* theme, led him in July, 1955 to conclude that "I have to write off much of the last 18 months as a dead loss, I fear." Two months before his death he wrote despairingly, "I am now writing a huge and sad novel about Burrard Inlet called *October Ferry to Gabriola* that I sometimes feel could have been better stated in about ten short poems — or even lines — instead."

"IT STARTS GENTLY, so gently" he wrote of *Ferry*'s beginning. Ethan and Jacqueline Llewelyn on the Greyhound bus are heading north to Nanaimo from Victoria, their dreams of a new home fed by retrospective flashbacks, a technique already employed in *Under the Volcano* and *Dark as the Grave*. A "retired" criminal lawyer of 39 and an ex-teacher of 31, the couple cosily anticipate a feedforward future, while biographical details drop carefully one by one into the reader's mind. Ethan won his last case only to learn that his client was really guilty. Jacqueline's father is Angus McCandless "of whom it was said, like Virgil, that he was a white magician." The couple met one another in 1938, in the foyer of a Toronto cinema where Douglas Fairbanks Jr. played in *Outward Bound*, a 1930 movie based on Sutton Vane's 1924 play.

The movie is a title for chapters 3 and 34 of *Ferry*, and, like *The Hands of Orlac* in *Under the Volcano*, a microcosmic metaphor for the book. In *Ultramarine* Dana Hilliot twice uses its title phrase: first he is on "the tramp steamer Oedipus Tyrannus, outward bound for hell"; but then at the book's end he is overjoyed "at last again to be outward bound, always outward, always onward," like Ahab an empty ship "outward bound". In both the movie and the play, *Outward Bound*, seven characters find themselves dead souls on a mysterious ship ferrying them from life to eternity, not knowing whether they will find hell or heaven at the end of their voyage. Among the seven are two young suicides who found an illicit love-life too hard to face, a sensitive drunkard and Scrubby the barman. The latter's parallel in *Ferry* whom he finds tending a bar in Nanaimo, turns out to be a person Ethan once successfully defended against a murder charge. It is probably no coincidence that Ethan's former client's name, Henry, is the same as that of the young male suicide.

The next film Ethan and Jacqueline saw together was *Isn't Life Wonderful,* in which two newly-married young lovers are driven from their hut-home on the forest's edge by looting soldiers. Eviction, one of *Ferry*'s main themes, is thus initially foreshadowed. By a perfect identification Ethan and Jacqueline become modern exemplars of the dispossessed lovers, who, as in *Outward Bound,* are reunited when the movie ends at the start of their long journey home. *Wuthering Heights,* the last film they have seen, portends the hate/love conflict that will temporarily split Ethan-Heathcliff from Jacqueline-Catherine.

Ethan is also cast as Ferdinand, Jacqueline as Miranda, with her father playing Prospero. McCandless is definitely based on Charles Stansfeld-Jones, Lowry's Cabbalistic mentor, who died in 1950. Lowry attended the funeral of his friend, who had served as "the mystical original-of-the Consul", as he admitted in a 1951 letter. Jacqueline is probably based upon the late Deirdre Stansfeld-Jones, Charles' adopted daughter, who was a great help in attending to Malcolm's burns after the Dollarton fire. Jacqueline's mother hanged herself in a gas-filled flat, as did Peter Cordwainer, Ethan's best friend at university, whose suicide will haunt the whole novel. Thus by the sixth of thirty-seven chapters the novel's end has been anticipated. It only remains for Ethan in a bar-parlour called "The Niagara" to comment on the eerie significance of cinemas in our life, as if they related to the after-life:

> and there had been too a certain indefinable sense of evil that this whole business of magic . . . seemed to evoke, as if, seated within this tavern of limbo, they at the same time inhabited some yet more shadowy realm, like Werner Kraus in *The Student of Prague,* both of them trapped there in a magic circle, which at the moment vacated by them, their places in the niche of the Ladies and Escorts, with its half-emptied glasses on the round table as if they were still invisibly seated there, must somewhat resemble.

In the "Niagara's" latrine, Peter Cordwainer's picture appears on the ads for Mother Gettle's Soups made by Cordwainer Products. A newspaper advertisement states that "Mother Gettle" was moving westward from London, to Quebec and to British Columbia. The threats of haunting continue as Ethan sees a boy on the bus with Peter's face. In Jacqueline's life-history Ethan sees a distorted reflection of his own. Angus McCandless, for example, is as guilty of the suicide of Jacqueline's real mother as he himself is of Peter's suicide. Yet as far as Angus's guilt is concerned, "he said that it was of less significance than as if a single hair had gone grey in God's eyebrow," even though he is both Jacqueline's adoptive and real father and she his bastard.

Slowly after eight chapters of flashback reflections we return temporarily to the bus, the Hound of Heaven no less, with the dead hand of the past controlling the "outward bound" passage of its occupants. For example, Ethan's first thoughts about the prospect of commuting by ferry from Gabriola Island to Nanaimo are "sad, a glum Charon's boat, plying up and down between mountains, the sun gleaming in the saloon windows: above, black clouds shot with bars of sunlight . . . And eternally bound as between some ultima thule and a nethermost suburb."

Uppermost in his thoughts are the recent threats of eviction from their house on piles built on Government-owned foreshore in the tiny village of Eridanus (Dollarton). Here since 1947 they had been extremely happy, "like spirits in some heaven of the Apocalypse or in some summerland of spiritualists, spirits who had no right to be where they were, which was their only source of doubt, when they doubted it." Expository material similar in tone to "The Forest Path to the Spring" follows, with Paradiso facing the encroaching Inferno of civilization. Simultaneously on the bus they pass a car with the sign SAFESIDE-SUICIDE on it, go through a village called My God Bay, where they pass a burned house; the My God Bay Society is commemorating Edgar Allen Poe's centenary, and there is a sign for Mother Gettle's Kettle Simmered Soup, M'mm, Good! etc. The Llewelyns' first house was in the country near Oakville, where Ethan could commute to Toronto. This had to be left when Mother Gettle put up a soup factory practically next door and industry began to move in. On the death of his father, Ethan inherited the old Llewelyn house in Niagara-on-the-Lake which suddenly and mysteriously burned to the ground while he and Jacqueline were away for a weekend in May, 1946, destroying everything save one item rescued by Jacqueline, a bottle of gin.

THE SECOND PART of *Ferry* begins with the Niagara-on-the-Lake chapter and its slipstream of thematic associations. Ethan identifies himself with Poe because both had attended Manor House School, a classical academy at Stoke Newington, near London. The Safeside-Suicide sign and the Mother Gettle advertisement recall Ethan's blame in not preventing Peter Cordwainer's suicide while the two were at college. Handing Peter a final drink of gin, Ethan had promised to follow his friend's example. Haunted ever by his role in "murder" by non-intervention, Ethan's career as a criminal lawyer has reminded him always of his own criminal Wandering Jew status. Another in this series of coincidences is the fact that Ixion (St. Catherine's) was both Ethan's college and the neighbouring town from which the Llewelyns returned to find their home razed.

From that day on began Ethan's obsessions with signs, portents and coincidences as evidence of continuing punishment and even damnation for his complicity twenty years prior to the day of the bus ride. If, to Angus McCandless, the whole thing was less to worry about than a grey hair in God's eyebrow, in Jacqueline, it provoked a far more perceptive insight:

> Yes, that he really had turned out a creature of hate, rather than of love; that the Heathcliff faction in his soul was real and abiding and implanted in his character — was not the most dishonest and plausible thing he had ever done to pretend to lay all the blame for this at the door of his own childhood? a character that hadn't been essentially mollified, for all the "goodness and kindness" of their marriage.

In chapter 17, "A House Where a Man Has Hanged Himself", Ethan consolidates her worst fears by assuming this role: "and now the windy whistling empty golf-links themselves with their blowing spiny spring grasses and sand dunes and stricken stunted thorn bushes like Wuthering Heights: 'I lingered round them, under that benign sky, watched the moths fluttering among the harebells'."

Chapters 18 to 21 are, as noted earlier, "self-contained". For the first time Ethan fully deserves his association with Hawthorne's plagued protagonist Ethan Brand, who likewise committed an Unpardonable Sin by separating mind and heart. Both men are linked with Cain, the Wandering Jew, Bunyan's *Pilgrim's Progress* and the threat of damnation. Ethan goes alone to see a movie of "The Wandering Jew", worrying initially that with his beard he might be mistaken for the main character, and then considering that "lo and behold, this movie might as well have been a sort of symbolic projection, phantasmagoria, of that life of yours, into which you'd come half-way through." ("Lo" is the title of one of Charles Fort's books, discussing ESP and the world of poltergeists.) For the first time in the novel Ethan's personality emerges as more than a tape-recorded case-history; admittedly, though, it is due to the allusive company it keeps. For a non-literary lawyer, Ethan is remarkably well-read: O'Neill, Dante, Eugene Sue, Dostoevsky, Booth Tarkington, Poe, Thurston, and especially Eino Railo, of whom more later. Where the allusions lie thickest, Lowry's manuscript marginalia comments honestly that the passage in point is far too done, too final and too pseudo-intellectual in its baffling purpose. Nevertheless, the accumulated effect aids the Law of Series, that "collision of contingencies" which relentlessly pursues Ethan from fire to fire, from Ontario to British Columbia.

A surprise visitor to the new home in Eridanus is Angus, who brings Eino Railo's unique study, *The Haunted Castle — A Study of the Elements of English Romanticism*, from which Ethan had drawn heavily in chapter 18. Unable to quote anything later than the early 19th century, Angus identifies parts of the Eridanus landscape by their counterparts in Spenser, Shelley, Mrs. Radcliffe, Coleridge and Shakespeare. Ethan widens his reading with a book on the Cabbala sent him by Angus,

> ... which, though its high-flown 'occult' diction struck him as peculiarly loathsome — bearing out one of its own theses that the higher a certain kind of mystic rose in such a hierarchy the more he was in danger of leaving his intelligence behind and his good taste as well — he found not only extraordinarily interesting, but as a method of thought, profoundly helpful. In fact he could sum up no better their life on the beach than to say it had been, in a manner, *his* cabbala, in the sense that, if he was not mistaken, that system might be regarded on one plane as a means less of accumulating than of divesting oneself — by arrangement, balancing them against their opposites — of unbalanced ideas: the mind, finally transcending both aspects, regains its lost equilibrium, or for the first time truly discovers it: not unlike, Ethan sometimes supposed, the modern process of psychoanalysis. "Rebirth" —

This process is put to the ultimate test in what is probably the book's most important chapter, "Useful Knots and How to Tie Them". The bus has drawn up at a grade crossing to let a log train pass with a load of very knotty wood. The rhythm of train wheels and windshield wipers respectively activate Ethan's hangover, alternately lulling and exacerbating him. Suddenly, out of the mist he sees a Mother Gettle's advertisement "showing a twenty times life-size cartoon of Peter, a lively, handsome, grinning youth of fifteen, gulping a great bowl of steaming soup and saying, "M'mmm, Good!'" Crying out, "That's the bloody last straw. We might just as well cut our throats now", Ethan experiences a destructively decomposing consciousness usurping the analytical legal "dossier" of his mind which he has been trying to order since boarding the bus that morning. Suddenly his mind is split between the counsel for its defence, the original consciousness, and now the counsel for the prosecution accusing him through the billboard picture of Peter, ironically an expert on knots. In a passage that recalls the George Eliot epigraph to the novel, Ethan reflects:

> This might actually be his soul with which he was not thinking, a soul that had become sick almost to death, that perhaps had been sold to the devil, a soul that could only plot the most merciless revenge on him for what he had done to it,

and that sick though it was, and speaking though it did partly with the accents of insanity, also spoke true.

(It is worth noting here that the probable springboard for this vital chapter was Cocteau's film *Orphée*, with its use of a grade-crossing as a death symbol and a pretty girl in a Rolls Royce as the Princess of Death. When the Lowrys left the theatre after seeing it the first thing that met their eye was a black Rolls-Royce.)

With the frantic beating of the railroad bell becoming the bells of the University of South Wales, exactly twenty years ago, Ethan is compelled to tell the whole story of that infamous night to Jacqueline. Compounding his associative guilt are echoes of "The Ancient Mariner" and Poe's "William Wilson".

Ethan had often been told he looked rather like Edgar Allen Poe... And his reflection in the rearview mirror, now opposite him, leaned forward, out of the past, as if to corroborate this. Yes, yes: there was the dark, the Byronic resemblance.... Suddenly he saw his whole life had been like one long malignant disease since Peter's death, ever since he'd forgotten it, forgotten it deliberately like a man who assures himself, after it begins to disappear, that the first lesion of syphilis is simply impetigo — like Thomas Mann's Dr. Faustus, in fact — forgotten it, or pretended to have forgotten it, and carried on as if nothing had happened. The face in the mirror, a half face, a mask, looked at him approvingly, smiling, but with a kind of half terror. Its lips silently formed the one word: Murderer!

The endlessly revised chapter ends with this passage, perhaps the most powerfully dramatic in the novel as Ethan's guilt and remorse are reborn through psychoanalysis prompted by coincidences in the Law of Series. In terms of Ethan's own Cabbala he is back in the Qliphoth, far from a state of Equilibrium. His deterioration cancerously spreads to Jacqueline who has also taken to drinking more lately, partly because she fears she can have no more children (they have one son, Tommy), and partly because of her former loneliness "in that Christ-awful god-forsaken hole" of Eridanus. To phrase it as succinctly as Lowry did, "both characters are hopped up to the gills." Both are also potential suicides unable to move as yet into the future symbolized by Gabriola Island, owing to the inexorable presence of the past. Looking ahead to the book's conclusion, Lowry employed two precise terms, *abreaction* and *cathexis*, to explain the all-pervading psychological preoccupation with the passed past. In psychoanalysis, *abreaction* is the relieving of a repressed emotion, as by talking about it. *Cathexis*, also a psychoanalytic term, is a concentration of psychic energy on particular persons, things, or ideas, such as Peter and Poe, suicide, damnation and eviction, all contained in time present.

Ethan's storm of self-confession is succeeded by the calm of the next chapter. Talking to cheer up Jacqueline, he suddenly feels that "everything seemed part of a miraculous plan, in which nothing stood still, everything good was capable of infinite development, everything evil must inevitably deteriorate." Therapeutic confession has temporarily united his soul; the self-division suggested by the novel's second epigraph is invisible for the moment at least. Arrival in Nanaimo distracts both sufferers from their former torments.

Awaiting the Gabriola ferry they overhear a sailor's remark that since he is English and married to an American girl, when he is outward bound he is homeward bound too:

> *"Outward bound ..."* the voice came from their first meeting, in the little movie theatre, in thunder and snow... *"But are we going to heaven or hell? But they are the same place, you see..."*
> Voyage, the homeward — outward — bound voyage; everybody was on such a voyage, the Ocean Spray, Gabriola, themselves, the barman, the sun, the reflections, the stacked glasses, even the light, the sea outside, now due to an accident of sun and dislimming cloud looking like a luminosity between two darknesses, a space between two immensities, was on such a voyage

Scrubby the barman is represented by the waiter, Henry Knight, whom Ethan defended in 1936 in Toronto, his first murder case. As one saved by Ethan from death, Henry partially counterweights Peter's suicide and thus boosts Ethan's confidence.

Invigorated after almost as much trouble in locating the Ferry as K had in finding The Castle, they are finally under way in the second chapter entitled "Outward Bound". Still, Ethan is slowly tempted to thoughts of suicide, ashamed partly by the gin bottle he is unable to open. Appalled by his lack of courage for life, he analyzes his motivation: "all his aspiration seemed to draw him back to a place he had not only already left, but on the acceptance of whose loss, and its transcending his very sanity appeared to depend." As an infantile fixation on the psychological plane, Eridanus has to be ultimately renounced. But for the time being Ethan thinks only that he has been deprived of his soul, another echo of the novel's first epigraph. Invoking the help of a priest, a fellow passenger, Ethan finds that even as a Protestant his confession would be heard. In tune again "with his destiny and that of the universe" he offers his gin to a woman who has just had her teeth removed and is haemorrhaging badly, so badly that the ferry has to return to Nanaimo. His altruism is rewarded by a newspaper headline ERIDANUS SQUATTERS REPRIEVED; as they read it, the ferry is once again bound for Gabriola, a highly significant reversal according to Lowry: "whereas before the ferry was a Charon boat proceeding to a kind of hell, now it is another sort of ferry, proceeding, as it were, toward the Mount of Purgatory (Mount Baker)." Gabriola becomes now the accepted future which imposes its own teleology on the destinies of Ethan and Jacqueline, who have individually been potentially reprieved from the remorse of self-destruction.

In the closing paragraphs the technique of the stars is borrowed from an idea of Flaubert's in *Herodias*. From a similar star formation Phanuel augured the death of a notable man that very night at Machaerus; unknown to him it was John the Baptist. Another parallel is seen but not wanted:

> How close this is in tone to the end of Conrad's *Youth* here. This is especially unfortunate because our idea is very different. With us our emotions have a different emotive value, and Gabriola is far more of a fructifying symbol than Conrad's of the far east.... It is possible that the story comes out of the same drawer of spiritual experience as *Youth* in a way hard to explain, and also from a similar unconscious drawer.... though on a different plane — there is the same symbolic use of fire — burning and purging away the rubbish of the past?

Lowry's explanation of the ending is prophetic:

> The end is a kind of Volcano in reverse and the final theme Faustian, with every-thing from flights of angels, balls of fire, and Madonnas, to the intervention of grace and the Himmelphart. The ferry reaches Gabriola at dusk, where those meeting the boat are swinging lanterns along the wharf: but you have the feeling that Ethan is now being received by mankind, that arms are stretched out to help him, help he now has to and is prepared to accept, as he is preparing to give help to man, whom he had formally grown to hate so much: thus the characters journey toward their own recovery. Something like that. I haven't told it very well. I'm sorry I'm late with it.

The novel has its ups and downs like the protagonists: excessively redundant exposition is the worst flaw; the development of the process of redemption is the highest accomplishment. Its drawbacks, as seen by Lowry, have been quoted earlier; its highlights are often the lyric passages worked and reworked to attain chatoyance. But with all said and done, I'm sure Margerie Lowry wishes over and again that Malcolm could have carried out his own imperative — that "one should write in the compositor's shop in the smell of printer's ink like Gautier, correcting it 10 pages at a time on the proofs themselves".   (1971)

INTERLUDE

SOME POEMS BY
MALCOLM LOWRY

Prefaced by Earle Birney

SCATTERED THROUGH THE MASS of typescript and manuscript left by Malcolm Lowry at his death, and now housed in the Special Collections section of the University of British Columbia Library, are various drafts or fragments of poems. A few of these were published during his lifetime, but about 150 were unknown. With the help of his widow, Mrs. Margerie Lowry, I have edited a selection of these with a view to their eventual publication as a book. The group printed below has been chosen from this work.

Since Lowry seldom dated poems, and habitually revised them, accumulating drafts indefinitely (as with most of his prose) it is not easy to arrange the present group in order of composition. From internal evidence, however, and from details supplied by Mrs. Lowry, it would appear that most of them were composed over the years between 1940 and 1954 when the Lowrys lived on the Dollarton beach, just beyond the upper harbour of Vancouver, except for three which may date, in their original conception, from the middle thirties, when Lowry lived in Mexico.

Of these three, "Autopsy"* (which exists, untitled, in one incomplete manuscript only), is of peculiar interest for the references it makes to incidents in his early years, incidents which he seldom openly referred to, but which appear to have been traumatic, and to recur in the prose in various symbolic disguises. According to Mrs. Lowry, his parents placed Malcolm in a boarding school at seven, where he was subjected to harsh discipline. He developed a disfiguring eye ailment, which was allowed to go without adequate treatment until he was in danger of blindness, and it was necessary for him to undergo an operation and

---

* Titles marked in this way have been added by Mrs. Lowry and Dr. Birney to poems untitled by the author. ED.

prolonged hospitalization. Lowry felt that both his parents and the school authorities were blameable for the aggravation of his condition, and he recalled also with bitterness that his ailment handicapped him in school sports and made him the butt of schoolmates. The phrase "crucified at eleven" may refer to the time when, at his father's insistence, he joined a Wolf Cub pack and underwent some form of sadistic bullying from older members. The reference to Clare, in the conclusion, I take to be to the "Summer Images" of John Clare in which that poet describes a snail as a "Frail brother of the morn, / That from the tiny bents and misted leaves / Withdraws his timid horn, / And fearful vision weaves."

"In Tempest's Tavern"*, also from the Mexican period, is one of a group Lowry called "Songs for Second Childhood". I should guess that the Dowson reference is to the opening section of Ernest Dowson's "Serephita". The Wordsworth reference is not so easy to place, though he may have had "Resolution and Independence" in mind, or the "Sonnet Composed during a Storm", or any of several passages in Dorothy Wordsworth's *Journals*. Lowry read fairly widely in nineteenth century poetry.

The title of the other poem dating from the Mexican period, "Lupus in Fabula"*, I have transferred from another poem to which it became accidentally attached and which it does not fit. The wolf became a complex symbol in Lowry's work, first of the cruelty of nature and of the "natural" man — I suspect the origin of this in the Wolf Cub experience — and later, by an interesting reversal, of the plight of all lonely creatures who cannot exist in modern society and are persecuted to extinction, including himself. "Tortu", according to the Consul in *Under the Volcano*, is a sort of Land of Cockayne containing "the ideal University", where "not even athletics is allowed to interfere with the business of . . . drinking." I would suppose that Lowry picked up the name when he visited Haiti in the forties, and that it was therefore not in the original draft. The nearest I can find to a Tortu is the Ile de la Tortue (Turtle Island) off the Haiti coast.

In 1942, *Under the Volcano* made an unsuccessful round of the publishers and was returned to Lowry by his agent with advice as to revision. According to Mrs. Lowry he at once set about rewriting it, while continuing to compose poems, including the "Joseph Conrad" published below. I do not know if Lowry was referring to a specific Conrad passage, but the opening lines seem to echo a sentence in *Typhoon*. Jukes, during the storm, is "harassed by the necessity of exerting a wrestling effort against a force trying to tear him away from his hold" — but Jukes is clinging to a stanchion, unable to get down to his bunk. In general the imagery and thought of the poem recalls Lowry's own *Ultramarine*, rather than anything of Conrad (even the famous preface to *The Nigger of the Narcissus*), and the title may have been, as Mrs. Lowry suspects, rather casually added.

In the summer of 1944, when the revision of the *Volcano* was almost complete, the squatter's shack in which the Lowrys were living burned to the ground; fortunately the *Volcano* manuscripts were rescued, but another unfinished novel, "In Ballast to the White Sea", was destroyed with all its notes. This is the event which prompted "Lament" (though the manuscripts reveal that he continued to revise this poem up to his death in 1957). With the help of neighbours, the Lowrys rebuilt their cabin, the *Volcano* was successfully revised, and, in 1946, accepted. "Strange Type"* was written in that year, when he was correcting proofs, and "After Publication . . ."* a year later, when he was already tasting the bittersweet of success.

The many painstaking redrafts of "Hypocrisy" suggest that it was a poem he considered important, but with which he was not satisfied. It probably refers to certain unhappy experiences he underwent when he first came to British Columbia and lived unwillingly in Vancouver until he could find a home on the beach.

"The Dodder" reflects the beginning of Lowry's interest in the natural world about him at Dollarton, though that interest was still, at this stage, a rather bookish one. In an endeavour to learn how to identify the local flowers he began reading *Studies of Plant Life in Canada*, a work by an amateur nineteenth-century botanist living at Katchewanook, near Stoney Lake, in eastern Ontario. Lowry's description of the dodder, and the other flower names and epithets in this poem, follow closely Mrs. Traill even though she is noting species which do not grow around Dollarton, or indeed in western Canada. Later, under his wife's tutelage, he grew more accurate in his botanizing. The poem is nevertheless revealing and moving for its symbolic application of Mrs. Traill's remarks to his feeling of dependence upon his wife and their life of "exiled passion" on the Dollarton beach. The general idea of the poem seems to me reminiscent of a sonnet of Conrad Aiken, the sixteenth in *And in the Human Heart*, (1940), a presentation copy of which was in Lowry's library on the beach. There are at least twenty-five drafts of this poem in the U.B.C. collection.

(1961)

A LAMENT - JUNE 1944

Our house is dead
It burned to the ground
On a morning in June
With a wind from the Sound.
The fire that fed
On our marriage bed
Left a bottle of gin.
Black under the moon
Our house is dead.
We shall build it again
But our home is gone.
And the world burns on.

IN TEMPEST'S TAVERN

Another than Wordsworth dropped his live work
To listen to the wind's shriek of uprooted trees,
And vessels smashed backs under portentous seas
Scrabbling with sharks as Rydal hives with bees,
The *Ohio* smoking in Frisco on a sharp pen
Of rock, lightning a leash snarled by force
At the bounding neck of God's mad dog, the dark;
The universe snapping like hounds at some dread groom.
I believe that Wordsworth thought of the calm . . .
But to another, blessing chaos, since it must drown
In hurled gules of conflict's flesh, his own strike
Of the hour, his own grief, no peaceful lake
Lights by storm's flash. Such is the nature of his doom
That like some infant Aeolus Dowson in tempest's tavern,
He claps for better thunder, wilder typhoon.

AFTER PUBLICATION OF "UNDER THE VOLCANO"

Success is like some horrible disaster
Worse than your house burning, the sounds of ruination
As the roof tree falls following each other faster
While you stand, the helpless witness of your damnation[.]

Fame like a drunkard consumes the house of the soul
Exposing that you have worked for only this—
Ah, that I had never suffered this treacherous kiss
And had been left in darkness forever to founder and fail[.]

HYPOCRISY

I sing the joy of poverty not such
As war insults with ruin of its own
Evil. But as the soul computes when much
Of its domain is lost. Here is a town
Of which one's sudden mayoralty
Prize of long kinship with disaster
Qualifies,—to readjust the dead.
Ideas stampede here, where are encamped
The hypocrite, the undertaker—yet, lo,
They are pitiable, and in different guise,
With hanging heads, melancholy.
And shall I tell them every one
Of the good of the soul scrubbed to the bone,
The walls bare of learning as the trees
Of leaves; and the sea—beyond—less bounded
For being innocent of ships.
What voices have they now, what forms of hopes?
What is the reckoning for having cheated death?
The Cross knows what I'll not say, that last never[.]
But no one shall heed my song, nor have they ever.

95

LUPUS IN FABULA

Wolf, wolf, cried the boy in the fable,
Who plagued the shepherds and the sheep alike,
To return, laughing softly, to the stable,
And fold away the hours with reed or fiddle,
Bleating in music for deceived shepherd's sake.
There was no wolf then. But at night one struck;
Long famished in iron hills she saw her table
Spread whitely on the green plains of Tortu.
Wolf, cried the boy. But now no herdsmen came.
Wolf, wolf, returned the wolf, her icy heart aflame . . .
So wolf and child were well met. But I say to you
That, slept they once on never so proud an Alp,—
It is the poor wolf now who cries for help.

THE DODDER

The early flowered everlasting,
The hooded violet, the branching white
Wood-violet, brooding in the May night
Send petals forth even in Spring's wasting,
—Sped by the monkish cellarage-tasting
Of cowled cuckoo-pint, jack-in-the-pulpit!—
All of these, where there was but one poet,
In Katchewanook, lacked no contrasting.
If I seek that which, poor, leafless, rootless,
Twined with goldenrod in ill-repute lives,
It is, for exiled passion's sake, comfort
Here, on Stony Lake: nor is it fruitless
What faithful coils are goldener than leaves
To share, what blossoms parasites support.

AUTOPSY

An autopsy on this childhood then reveals:
That he was flayed at seven, crucified at eleven.
And he was blind as well, and jeered at
For his blindness. Small wonder that the man
Is embittered and full of hate, but wait.
All this time, and always lost, he struggled.
In pain he prayed that none other
In the world should suffer so. Christ's
Life compared with his, was full of tumult,
Praise, excitement, final triumph.
For him were no hosannas. He writes them now.
Matriculated into life by this, remembering how
This laggard self was last in the school Marathon,
Or that he was last, last in everything,
Devoid of all save wandering attention—
Wandering is the word defines our man—
But turned, to discover Clare in the poor snail,
And weave a fearful vision of his own.

STRANGE TYPE

I wrote: in the dark cavern of our birth.
The printer had it tavern, which seems better:
But herein lies the subject of our mirth,
Since on the next page death appears as dearth.
So it may be that God's word was distraction,
Which to our strange type appears destruction,
Which is bitter.

JOSEPH CONRAD

This wrestling, as of seamen with a storm
Which flies to leeward—while they, united
In that chaos, turn, each on his nighted
Bunk, to dream of chaos again, or home—
The poet himself, struggling with the form
Of his coiled work, knows; having requited
Sea-weariness with purpose, invited
What derricks of the soul plunge in his room.
Yet some mariner's ferment in his blood
—Though truant heart will hear the iron travail
And song of ships that ride their easting down—
Sustains him to subdue or be subdued.
In sleep all night he grapples with a sail!
But words beyond the life of ships dream on.

PART II

The Man and the Sources

MALCOLM LOWRY

A Note

Conrad Aiken

MY OPINION OF MALCOLM LOWRY as a writer is of course already on record, in the "blurb" which I was asked to write for *Under the Volcano* when it first appeared. More extensively, it can be found in the portrait of Lowry—on the whole, pretty accurate—in *Ushant*, my autobiography, where he appears as Hambo. In the last section of this is a fragment of imaginary dialogue between us which was actually written at Cuernavaca in 1937, when I was staying with him, and which, allowing for the necessary "heightening", is very close to the mark. It will suggest, I think, something of the remarkable spiritual and aesthetic and psychological symbiosis that grew up between us immediately after our first meeting in 1929. He had read my novel *Blue Voyage*, and wrote me about it to Rye, Sussex, where he assumed I was still living; and he asked me to lunch with him, either in London or Cambridge, where he was to matriculate in September. On finding that I was in the *other* Cambridge — on the Charles River — he at once inquired whether I would consider taking him on as a pupil, the terms to be arranged. The terms were arranged, he set sail on a freighter from Liverpool to Bermuda, on another from Bermuda to Boston, and arrived one day in July on my doorstep in Plympton Street, Cambridge, next door to the Grolier Bookshop, with a taropatch in one hand and a small battered suitcase in the other.

The suitcase contained an exercise book (and not much else) in which was as much as he had then written of his first novel, *Ultramarine*; and it was on this, as I have described at length in *Ushant*, that we were to work all that wonderful summer. *Blue Voyage* he knew better than I did — he knew it by heart. Its influence on him was profound and permanent, and was evident even in that first title — he was delighted with my suggestion that he might well have taken the next step and called the book *Purple Passage*. But though the influence was to continue even into the later work, a matter that was frequently and amusedly discussed between us, and was also to comprise a great deal that was said by me in conversation, it was much more complicated than that. The fact is that we were uncannily alike in almost everything, found instantly that we spoke the same language, were astonishingly *en rapport*; and it was therefore the most natural thing in the world that a year later, when difficulties arose between him and his father, I was able to act as mediator (I had by then returned to Rye), and, as a result of this, for the next three years, in *loco parentis*. I became his father.

Time and space were to interrupt this quite marvellous relationship, but never to change it. *Tout passe, l'amitié reste.* His first letter to me had begun: "I have lived only nineteen years, most of them badly." Would he have thought that he lived the *rest* of his short life badly? No, I don't think so. The work speaks for him, and he knew that it was superb.

(1961)

LOWRY'S LETTERS

Hilda Thomas

> *La Nature est un temple où de vivant piliers*
> *Luissent parfois sortir de confuses paroles,*
> *L'homme y passe à travers des forêts de symboles*
> *Qui l'observent avec des regards familiers.*
>
> *Charles Baudelaire*

"LOWRY IS QUITE LUCID about what is sickness and what is health," says Robert Heilman in his article "The Possessed Artist and the Ailing Soul". The *Selected Letters of Malcolm Lowry*, edited by Harvey Breit and Margerie Bonner Lowry, provide a valuable affirmation of both the lucidity and the essential good health of their author. Lowry lived for fifteen years the somewhat benighted existence of a remittance man, struggling with both hell and highwater in his squatter's shack on the shore of Burrard Inlet. Here he produced the bulk of his work, beginning with the final draft of *Under the Volcano*. But even before his death Lowry had begun to be identified in legendary fashion with the central character of his novel. The legend was encouraged by Lowry's occasional public drinking bouts; at times he seemed deliberately to play the role of his self-destroying hero. But the *Letters* show him to be at once more robust and more cheerful — healthier both physically and spiritually — than the Consul. What is even more important, the *Letters* offer evidence of what even some of his most admiring critics have been slow to grant him: that Lowry was a scrupulous craftsman, attentive to the smallest details of his composition, and engaged in a continuous effort to discover the form exactly appropriate to his material.

The most important single item in the collection is the letter addressed to Jonathan Cape from Cuernavaca, January 2, 1946. Here, in a sustained and coherent essay, Lowry answers the criticisms of the publisher's reader, offering a chapter-by-chapter analysis of *Under the Volcano*. The report to which Lowry is replying is not included in the *Selected Letters*. Perhaps it is not available, or perhaps it was omitted to spare its writer the embarrassment of having cavilled at a masterpiece. But Lowry freely admits the reasonableness, if not the ultimate validity, of the reader's criticisms, and he takes great pains to vindicate what appeared to be the chief defects in his novel: the unusually long and slow-paced opening chapter, the weakness of the character drawing, and the over-elaborate style.

Of chapter one he writes,

> ...I suggest that whether or not the *Volcano* as it is seems tedious at the beginning depends somewhat on that reader's state of mind and how prepared he is to grapple with the form of the book and the author's true intention...
> — if he were *conditioned*, I say, ever so slightly towards the acceptance of that slow beginning as inevitable, supposing I convince you it is — slow, but perhaps not necessarily so tedious after all — the results might be surprising. ... I feel the first chapter... is necessary since it sets... the mood and tone of the book as well as the slow melancholy tragic rhythm of Mexico itself — its sadness — and above all establishes the *terrain*....

Later he refers to the novel as ". . . a kind of symphony, or in another way as a kind of opera — or even a horse opera. It is hot music, a poem, a song, a tragedy, a comedy, a farce, and so forth." Lowry's intentional grasp of his material, and his critical judgement, are confirmed — if confirmation is needed — by the response of at least one critic. In his brief article on *Under the Volcano*, "No Se Puede...", Max-Pol Fouchet has this to say about the first chapter:

> Défaut de composition? Non pas. Procédé trop intentionnel? Encore moins. Il s'agit de quelques autres choses. De musique, d'abord, si l'on veut. Ce premier chapitre, purgatoire des impatients, équivaut à un prélude; les leitmotifs s'y font entendre, sans qu'on sache encore à quel événement précis les rattacher. L'oeuvre de Malcolm Lowry, en effet, ressemble à une symphonie dont les motifs, par leur récurrence, assurent l'unité tonale, se reprennent en modulations, s'organisent parfois en contrepoint. C'est aussi un poème, où ces thèmes tiennent lieu de rimes, d'assonances.

Lowry's discussion of character in *Under the Volcano* is of particular interest, for it contains the seeds of his growing preoccupation with Ortega's idea that "the best image for man himself *is* a novelist...." He says, "character was my last consideration as it was Aristotle's — since there isn't *room*, for one thing." Citing Sean O'Faolain as the source of "this heretical notion" he goes on,

The novel then . . . should reform itself by drawing upon its ancient Aeschylean and tragic heritage. There are a thousand writers who can draw adequate characters till all is blue for one who can tell you anything new about hell fire. And I am telling you something new about hell fire. I see the pitfalls — it can be an easy way out of hard work, an invitation to eccentric word-spinning, and laboured phantasmagorias, and subjective inferior masterpieces that on closer investigation turn out not even to be bona fide documents but like my own *Ultramarine*, to be apparently translated with a windmill out of the unoriginal Latvian, but just the same in our Elizabethan days we used to have at least passionate poetic writing about things that will always mean something. . . : and in this sense I am trying to remedy a deficiency, to strike a blow, to fire a shot for you as it were, roughly in the direction, say, of another Renaissance: it will probably go straight through my brain but that is another matter.

Earlier in the same letter he has spoken of being "in rebellion, both revolutionary and reactionary at once" against the kind of novel most critics admire. He is reactionary, Lowry seems to be saying, in that he took great pains to provide even the simplest reader with an adequate story, his approach in this respect "being opposite . . . to that of Mr. Joyce, i.e., a simplifying [sic] as far as possible, of what originally suggested itself in far more baffling, complex and esoteric terms, rather than the other way round." The rebellion is in the direction of what Lowry was to describe much later (in 1953) as "a new form, a new approach to reality itself. . . ."

THE EVOLUTION OF LOWRY'S STYLE is inseparably bound up with his struggle to find the form appropriate to a new approach to reality. He recognized that in *Under the Volcano*, "the constant repetition of churrigueresque", of an overloaded style "seemed to be a suggestion that the book was satirizing itself." But a simpler style would not have supported the complexity of Lowry's subject, which is nothing less than the fall of man, and his painful and seemingly futile effort to redeem himself. Lowry realized that the subject was too large for a single novel. In 1940-41, he explains to Albert Erskine, he

conceived the idea of a trilogy entitled *The Voyage That Never Ends* . . . (nothing less than a trilogy would do) with the *Volcano* as the first, infernal part, . . . the whole to concern the battering the human spirit takes (doubtless because it is overreaching itself) in its ascent towards its true purpose.

The trilogy was never completed, doubtless because Lowry, too, was overreaching himself, but also because he was constantly reassessing his material. As George Woodcock puts it, in "Under Seymour Mountain", he

> revised and added to his Work in Progress as the result, not of remembering a past now dead, but of experiencing and incorporating a lived present.

The lived present for Lowry during most of his productive years meant Eridanus, the cabin on the bank of Burrard Inlet which provided the setting for "The Forest Path to the Spring", described in one of his letters as a story about "human integration". It meant also a struggle for personal integration, carried out in the face of a disastrous fire, the constant threat of eviction ("We evict those who destroy!"), winter of unprecedented severity ("the elements are following us around"), and a series of illnesses and accidents seemingly designed to confirm Lowry's view of the world as "a kind of gruesome and serious absurdity". But "cheerfulness is always breaking in," as he wrote to Conrad Aiken. It breaks in to the *Letters* in the form of outrageous puns, hilarious descriptions of nearly fatal accidents, and warm words of encouragement addressed alike to old friends and bare acquaintances. Without the *Letters* it would be difficult to imagine Lowry accompanying himself on a taropatch while he sang songs he wrote himself, or building a pier (and, incidentally, an outhouse), or writing the line, "to what wild centuries roves back the contorted louse-wort?" Without the *Letters*, in other words, it would be difficult not to confuse Lowry with the Consul. Most of the letters were written from Dollarton.

Dollarton was Lowry's "Place where you know". Each time he left it his daemon failed him — overcome as often as not by that other demon, rum — or he was beset by unimaginable difficulties. Lowry's account of the way he and his wife were treated by officials when they went to Mexico in 1946 "to spend the winter for purposes of travel and health" reads like a Hitchcock version of a novel by Franz Kafka. A letter written to Albert Erskine from France in the summer of 1948 give a pretty clear idea of the state of his mind at that time. He writes:

> I have to confess, however, that in spite of this comparatively lucid burst of correspondence, that I am going steadily & even beautifully downhill: my memory misses beats at every moment, & my mornings are on all fours. Turning the whole business round in a nutshell I am only sober or merry in a whisky bottle, & since whisky is impossible to procure you can imagine how merry I am, & lucid, & by Christ I am lucid. And merry. But Jesus. The trouble is, apart from Self, that part (which) used to be called: consciousness. I have now reached a position where

every night I write 5 novels in imagination, have total recall (whatever that means too) but am unable to write a word.

When he returned to Dollarton in 1949, Lowry entered on a sustained creative period which lasted, in spite of broken bones, a severed artery, hurricanes, toothache, etc., etc., until he left Canada in 1954. He wrote from detailed notes taken during the Mexican holiday, the voyage through the Panama, and the year spent in Europe — notes which suggest that he must in fact have been sober and lucid and merry at least part of the time — working simultaneously on several novels and on the short stories which were published after his death in the volume *Hear Us O Lord From Heaven Thy Dwelling Place*.

Hear Us O Lord was conceived as a series of twelve stories which "would be, if done aright, less a book of short stories than — God help us — yet *another* kind of novel: a kind of ... *Volcano* in reverse, with a triumphant ending...." He had described just such a novel thirteen years earlier in a letter to James Stern:

It is possible to compose a satisfactory work of art by the simple process of writing a series of good short stories, complete in themselves, with the same characters, interrelated, correlated, good if held up to the light, watertight if held upside down, but full of effects and dissonances that are impossible in a short story, but nevertheless having its purity of form, a purity that can only be achieved by the born short-story writer.... (And I don't mean the kind of novel...in which the preoccupation with form vitiates the substance, that is by a writer whose inability to find a satisfactory form for his poems drives him to find an outlet for it in the novel.) No. The thing that I mean can only be done by a good short-story writer, who is generally the best kind of poet, the one who only does not write poetry because life does not frame itself kindly for him in iambic pentametres and to whom disjunct experimental forms are abhorrent...my thesis is that he is capable of writing the best kind of novel, something that is bald and winnowed, like Sibelius, and that makes an odd but splendid din, like Bix Beiderbecke.

In 1953 Lowry was still trying to find a satisfactory form for his own work, but the complexity of his theme and the very nature of his conception of character posed an insoluble problem. He continued to think in terms of a series of works, each, like *Under the Volcano*, an entity complete in itself, but each to have a place in a larger unity called *The Voyage That Never Ends*. The whole would consist of *Under the Volcano, Hear Us O Lord*, and three novels: *Dark as the Grave, La Mordida*, and *October Ferry to Gabriola*. "The real protagonist of the *Voyage*," he wrote in a letter to Albert Erskine, "is not so much a man or a writer as the unconscious — or man's unconscious. . . ." Sigbjørn Wilderness, the hero of the three novels, is "Ortega's fellow, making up his life as he goes along. . . ."

> What he suspects is that he's not a writer so much as being *written* — this is where the terror comes in. (It came in, just then.) His tragedy or his fable or whatever is less that of Faust than that of Aylmar, the water-diviner . . . a character of the Middle Ages who, with his wand, was used by the French authorities to track down murderers; half fake, because his talent kept failing at embarrassing moments, wouldn't work at all under certain conditions, yet he had to pretend it *was* working; half genius, because he nearly always got his man. . . .

The resemblance to Lowry himself is obvious; but Lowry was writing fiction, not autobiography. He was trying to find a form which would contain his immense and paradoxical theme. Setting aside *Dark as the Grave*, which consisted of "700 pages of notes and drafts . . . not in a fit state to read," and *La Mordida*, which had been "started on the long haul of typing", he turned to the third novel, *October Ferry to Gabriola*. He was still in possession, if not in control, of his daemon:

> . . . — I have willed one thing and the daemon has decided another. . . . I can master my booze, my bad temper, my self-deceit, and to some extent my other myriad bad habits, but I have not learned how to master that bugger. And if he was a good one it would be different. But he is slow, confused, paranoiac, gruesome of mind, as well as being completely implacable, and he seems to have some vices unknown even to me. And in *Gabriola* he has turned what set out to be an innocent and beautiful story of human longing into quite one of the most guilt-laden and in places quite Satanically horrendous documents it has ever been my unfortunate lot to read, let alone have to imagine I wrote. One saving grace is that it is in places incredibly funny. . . .

The implacable daemon was never to be subdued. In August of 1954 the Lowrys left Dollarton, the work still unfinished. They spent the winter in Taormina (which Lowry hated) and went from there to England where, on June 27, 1957, he died. Coroner's verdict: Death by Misadventure.

The *Selected Letters* afford much insight into the challenge Lowry set himself as an artist, and the agonies he endured as he wrestled with the problem of integration in his work and in his life. Perhaps in Sussex he could have achieved the distance, the retrospective detachment, that would have enabled him to bring his endless *Voyage* to a close. The name of the village in which he settled — Ripe

— must at least have pleased and encouraged him. Or perhaps, after all, it would have proved impossible to find the formal resolution for a work which was constantly being reshaped by the author's own experience — or, more precisely, *reinvented* as the author invented his own life. Ortega's idea, he wrote to his friend Downie Kirk in 1950,

> probably recommends itself to me partly because if it is true, and man is a sort of novelist of himself, I can see something philosophically valuable in attempting to set down what actually happens in a novelist's mind when he conceives what he conceives to be the fanciful figure of a personage, etc., for this, the part that never gets written ... would be the true drama. ...

The question is unanswerable. But the *Letters* allow us at least to measure Lowry's posthumously published work against the author's intention. And they allow us to measure the man himself against the characters he invented, and to find that he is, indeed, the Consul; but he is also Hugh, and Laruelle, and Sigbjørn Wilderness, and many other wondrous things besides. He *was* incredibly funny. He was also incredibly kind and generous, a man of great humility and an artist of genius. "Life is a forest of symbols," he wrote to Erskine in 1946. And Lowry was attentive to every tree along his forest path. Only a few days before he died he wrote to David Markson,

> Do you know which stars are which and what bird is flying over your head and what flower blossoming? If you don't the anguish of not knowing is a very valid field for the artist. Moreover when you learn something it's a good thing to repossess the position of your original ignorance.

Lowry's humble regard for the natural world, which, with the help of his wife, he learned to know in its minutest details, is reflected in the *Letters*, as it is in all his work. For a few years he found in Eridanus the earthly paradise he sought, and there he created one of the great novels of this century, a profound and visionary expression of man's despair and his hope.

(1971)

TWO LETTERS

Malcolm Lowry

TO ALBERT ERSKINE

DOLLARTON (1946)

Dear Mr. Erskine:

Well, every man his own Laocoon!

Concerning a letter forwarded me yesterday by Hal Matson, about your having postponed the VOLCANO I wrote you one asking you if it was still not too late to change your mind without doubtless taking fully into account that it was the amount of research I seemed calmly suggesting you do, quite apart from the number of corrections I was making myself, not to say insertions, many of which may have appeared to you quite negligible, that had been responsible for the postponement.

On top of these items I perceive clearly the paradox of Cape tying up the Canadian rights with the obligation if you bring the book out this year while your author meantime makes it quietly and maddeningly impossible for you to do this.

I did not of course make any such suggestion to Cape myself, but so far as that goes I'm writing him anyhow on the subject and I'm sure he'll waive the stipulation. I have no British agent at the present. I should have had Hal's representative act for me over there, but the insane coincidence of getting the news of the book's acceptance on the same day in two countries at once was enough to ravel any author into knots.

For myself the delay has been caused by the arrival of the MSS from Mexico, as well as by second thoughts due to my recent visit there, the awful difficulty of getting books here, the non-existence of our own owing to the fire, and numerous other difficulties I won't go into, but which, all piling up at once at this point, make me believe in Cocteau's remark, "Truly, our books hate us."

For the rest, while I am proud of having written UNDER THE VOLCANO, I must confess to being slightly tremulous of it. I have not been fortunate, to say the least, in my work so far and it would distress me to think you were losing interest in it so soon after you had seemed to have such high hopes for it.

There are really no echoes etc. that I do not myself really consider to be absolutely justifiable and assimilated, *absorbed*, and I have mentioned them to you partly for my own psychological benefit and partly in case you might, somehow, disagree.

I will not now make these the subject of a separate appendix to my notes but when I come to any either coincidental or otherwise will simply mention it and the page in question, since I feel you should know of their existence.

Enclosed are notes on IV. There is nothing in V to speak of save the Jardin problem, already solved, nothing in VI I can see now save the German to be verified, nothing in VII save a little Spanish and the garden again, in VIII little, IX nothing at all unless you consider something, in X I'll try to cut somewhat, and nothing to speak of in XI or XII.

This may still, I am aware, leave too much for you to do to get it out by October, but I hate to let you down, if that is what I seem to be doing, and am willing and ready to cooperate wherever and however I can. In either case, would you give me a deadline? I seem to remember there is one on the contract but I have no copy of it.

Chapter V

p. 128. Significance of "interlube" has passed from my mind. But it might have something to do with the London Daily Herald or the United Press, if that matters. Cable is based on real one and used by permission of the reporter who sent it I having sat in at the concoction thereof. Cable was, until lately, in my possession.

p. 129. For Bill H. — substitute Bill Hod.

p. 130. in brackets "for he was secretly enormously etc." please cut the for.

p. 134. After sentence beginning: Unconsciously he had been watching her, please place comma after "arms", cut "against" and place another comma after "slacks."

p. 137. typografical error: emanate.

p. 138. Man with a dog named Harpo, is partly old pal of mine, John "Volunteer in Spain" Summerfield, who survived after all. De Quincey incident mentioned in *Volunteer in Spain*, likewise in letter to me at that time. I don't see how anyone could be hurt, least of all John, who painted a wild portrait of me in his novel, The Last Week End (not to be confused with Lost) published in London. De Quincey comes in also because of Mr. Quincey and the knocking at the gate bit in V.

p. 140.   In the middle I would have cut Yvonne's dialogue at "saying that you wanted —" and have Hugh interrupt at that point without any "Hugh answered". It remains as it is as a concession to the reader.

p. 143.   "You've got your cattle again I see," Yvonne said in a bracket. It is a technical echo of something in Faulkner's *Wild Palms*, I think in a similar bracket, "There's your horse again," she said, or something. The trouble about acknowledging such a thing, it embarrasses the embarrassee yet somewhere else.

p. 144.   top. In Yvonne's dialogue, please insert the word "together" between ridden and before.

p. 145.   Please verify Spanish at top. I think it's O.K.

ibid. At the end of the first long paragraph, after shadow his brother everywhere, please cut dots.

147.   Ejido. Please verify. I'm pretty certain it's right.

p. 150.   Las Manos de Orlac.

p. 152.   This Judas passage was written before I had read Dorothy Wellesley's poem in Yeats Oxford book of Modern Verse, where she likewise speaks of Judas having a hangover. Any resemblance is purely coincidental.

p. 154.   In bottom paragraph semicolon after machinery was intentional but if you changed it to a comma that's O.K. by me.

p. 163.   *Buy* one, please give this a question mark

p. 164.   Please change Bab-el-Mandeb to Arabian Sea.

p. 171.   ditto.

(UNSIGNED)[1]

TO DAVID MARKSON

DOLLARTON, BRITISH COLUMBIA
CANADA, JUNE 20, 1951.
(OWING TO MORE "AUXILIARY CIRCUMSTANCES")

Dear David Markson:

I thank you sincerely for your letter, the remarks therein, and the honour you do me.

As I said the least I can do is to see if I can lighten at all such a formidable chore for you in a hot summer, especially since my name means "servant of Colomb" and we have two Columbias in the address not to mention a selva,[2] if not oscura, while we literally do live in a forest, or rather at the edge of one.

Moreover just as I received your letter I too seemed to have been reading a bit of Faulkner hotly pursued by Djuna Barnes, Dante, Joyce, etc., and feeling frightened by *my* limitations — incidentally, if I may say so in a tone of complete joviality and politeness you made a wonderful type error, unless it was done on purpose at this point: you said "freightened". Now I only remark this because having begun this letter in pencil I went on to use it to introduce my apology, viz, that our typewriter was then lying at a garage having its inner workings cleansed by an aeolian instrument for blowing up tires: so, writing as I do now in pencil I did not lay myself open to such type-errors — if I do now, all I can say is, may they be as good as that one of yours! For you said a mouthful. If your vocation is to be a novelist you certainly couldn't do better — in my sincere if by no means new opinion — than to be "freightened" rather than "frightened" by the said limitations: one should (upon the "frighter" of life) take them to Palembang with one and deliver them in good order as may be — after all they can be among the most valuable cargo one has, those limitations! Though I don't mean quite to say as Melville somewhere marvellously puts it — one should "never wait for fair weather, which never was on land or sea, but dash with all one's derangements at one's object, leaving the rest to fortune." Not quite; very unsound advice: though it may be very necessary at times.

But this is not answering any of your questions. Re those, I think the most helpful thing I can do at the moment is to send you — it will go off by the same post as this letter — a copy of the French translation of Under the Volcano which contains a preface written by myself, as also a postface written by someone else, so many faces indeed that instead of being much help they probably serve to the contrary as so many masks over the material. This preface was written in Haiti — or going there — and was originally intended for the British edition. (You will note that I received news of the acceptance of the Volcano from England and America, upon the same day, delivered by a *character* in the Volcano, and in a house that figures in the Volcano, in Mexico itself, where ten years after I'd begun the book we went back on a short visit — the original of Laruelle's house I'd never set foot in before, was now turned into apartments: the very tower described in the Volcano was the only place we could find to live — this sort of thing — a sort of Under Under the Volcano or fantasia of the Law of Series or the History of Peter Rabbit's imagination — E. M. Forster says someone should write the history of someone's imagination — is roughly the theme of what I'm working on now and one day hope to complete — I had some setbacks as you will see — who doesn't?)

In this preface also I go on about the Kabbala in a way that is — in this case — quite misleading and probably not a little juvenile, and which was no doubt suggested by the magnificently abyssal and heavenly motions of one of your bauxite freighters on which the preface was written, rather than in strict fact. Moreover we had probably been drinking rum with the skipper, not to say listening to the voodoo drums battering and tambouring and otherwise genekrupaering along that inlet when you begin to sail into that Heart of Lightness and Tightness and Barbancourt and Cinq Etoiles. It is true that the Kabbala played a part, though scarcely anterior to the fact of writing the book; I mean I didn't group it *consciously* around any of the correspondence within that unresting and dynamic cabinet-cum-tree of knowledge. But that I ran into a Kaballist at a critical and coincidental moment in the writing of the book: that is true, right in this forest also. But apart from that my remarks here — though not the other remarks I have cited — can be taken about on a par with Sanarelle's Latin:

Sanarelle (assuming various comic attitudes) Cabricias arci thuram, catalamus, singulariter, nominativo, haec musa, the muse, bonus bona bonum Deus sanctus, este oratio latinas? Etiam, Yes. Quare? Why.

Geronte: Ah! Why did I not study?

Jacqueline: What a clever man!

It might have been more honestly to the point if I'd mentioned the influence of Bismarck — to wit Bix Beiderbecke — especially a break in Singing the Blues in an old Frankie Trumbauer record, in that preface — but it appears I like to be thought erudite: the truth is other; I have the kind of mind that is sometimes politely called archaic, it is true, but not in the sense that it is on really fraternal terms with the scholastics and medieval philosophy.

Subjective, stream of consciousness, multi-leveled and symbolic. Yes, indeed, but this is too symbolic, multi-leveled, conscious and subjective a matter for me to speak about in a short letter in a way which would be much use to you.

Joyce, Dante, Djuna Barnes, Faulkner. Of these I'm not really qualified to speak either, though I'll try and reply to anything, should you ask me any specific questions. I think there are certain writers who in youth tend to react against anything like a ready-made tradition, or the suspicion that teachers or another poet taught may be foisting a tradition upon me for reasons of their own; thereafter they approach these recommended writers tentatively, preferably when they have fallen into more disrepute. Meantime the writers the writer feels *he* has discovered for himself remain the more valuable. I know that's more or less true of me.

Re Joyce and Djuna Barnes I find myself ungratefully inclining a bit to Leavis' distaff view on The Great Tradition (even though he is trying to impose a tradition and is dealing with the English tradition of novelists. But this is a valuable book if only it encourages you to read George Eliot's Middlemarch.) I've never grappled with the whole plan of Faulkner yet, though I mean to. I didn't realize for myself what a tremendous writer he was at his best until fairly recently. (Dante's still a bit too famous for me, though you caught me reading him on the sly, when your letter arrived.)

Ultramarine is very fortunately out of print (was never really printed as it was meant to be) and is an absolute flop and abortion and of no interest to you unless you want to hurt my feelings. As my brother said to me recently when I mildly suggested to him that the British Government owed me some cash — "Don't even speak of it to me!" However I mean to rewrite it — or rather to write it — one day. A later work, *Lunar Caustic* — not yet published in America because I wanted to rewrite it but I believe to be published in France as it stands — is maybe of more interest; anyway I think it's good. Unfortunately I haven't got a spare copy to send you, but maybe I can tell you what you want to know about it. You'll find some mention of the general plan in the French preface which fundamentally has not been abandoned.

My wife — who is American — wrote a grand book called *Horse in the Sky* which was very unfairly neglected and should cognately interest you — we swop horses and archetypes with each other all the time. She has just finished another much better book even than this, which I certainly feel you will hear of.

I also have had the great privilege of being one of Conrad Aiken's oldest friends. Him I have known since my teens and the good old days of bathtub gin and the best and most helpful of fellows he is.

I am reading at the moment *The Road to Damascus* by Strindberg . . . By the well a large tortoise. On right, entrance below to a wine cellar. An icechest and dust bin. The doctor enters from the verandah with a telegram playing a long range ukulele, etc. . . .

We live an extremely sunfilled and seay life between the beach — and I mean the beach — and the forest here and if you're ever in these parts I hope you'll look us up and have a drink and some sun with us.

With kindest regards and the best of luck,

MALCOLM LOWRY

P.S. Of course send along any of your MSS you wish to and I'll make any helpful comments I can.

FOOTNOTES

[1] Margerie Lowry comments: "I can only suppose that since he went directly from the letter into the notes and comments he must have thought he'd signed the letter and he didn't. I can't think of any other reason."

[2] At this time David Markson was attending Columbia University.

MORE THAN MUSIC

The Critic as Correspondent

Downie Kirk

Sir, more than kisses, letters mingle souls;
For, thus friends absent speak.

JOHN DONNE

IT WOULD TAKE a symposium of the friends with whom Malcolm Lowry corresponded to describe him adequately from his letters. Yet, one correspondent, basing his impressions upon letters which were written during the decade that was the most productive period of his literary career, can still give a significant view of the man and the artist. One naturally wonders, of course, what right one really has to quote from the private letters of an author; one is sharply reminded of Heine's remark: "To publish even one line of an author which he himself has not intended for the public at large — especially letters which are addressed to private persons — is to commit a despicable act of felony."

But in the case of Malcolm Lowry one may perhaps be pardoned, for obviously some of the care that made him revise almost every paragraph he wrote, went into the composition of his letters, although it is doubtful that he wrote them with a view to publication. In fact, it is their very naturalness that makes them valuable. He obviously wrote many of them under pressure, at a time when he was absorbed in the composition of his novels and his poetry; for he makes frequent references to the long stretches of strain caused by his creative work, in the midst of which he would write a letter in reply to an invitation to spend an evening of complete relaxation from his creative endeavours.

> When I'm working at very high intensity [he says on one occasion] the writing of even the smallest note often takes an incredibly long time—an occupational psychological abberration of some sort doubtless due in turn to the fact that the narcissistic care which one sometimes expends on prose makes a fellow forget a letter should be spontaneous and to hell with the semicolons, since your friend doesn't want to look at them anyway but is simply interested in hearing from you.

Joseph Conrad once said that he could compare the strain of writing *Nostromo* only to the everlasting sombre stress of the westward winter passage around Cape Horn. So it must have been with Malcolm Lowry; for he drove himself mercilessly to produce his works: with him there was a passionate necessity to reflect and to distil in its purest form something within him that would not give him peace. And many of the letters — "the only true heart-talkers," as someone has said — are as revelatory of Lowry as his autobiographical fiction. The expression of his thought is neither cryptic nor obscure. His commentary on life and literature is all the more precious because it is good vivid talk by the Lowry whom not many could listen to with complete comprehension for any length of time because of the abstruseness of his references and the broad leaps in his thoughts. He was, of course, shy, and although he was dying to communicate, he often remained silent; when he did open his mouth, it was to release a flood of words that dazzled you with its brilliance but frequently left you bewildered about its meaning.

We are now aware of Malcolm Lowry as an outstanding novelist, as a distinguished short-story writer and as a considerable poet, but his power as a critic is practically unknown. His book reviews and literary criticisms, although not numerous, are penetrating. His letters, moreover, reveal him as a sensitive critic of literature, politics, music, art and philosophy; in them he discusses with acute perception and in clear style a wide range of unusual subjects.

In one letter he tells about reading José Ortega y Gasset — especially his wonderful lecture on Goethe, and his *Towards a Philosophy of History*. In the latter work the Spanish philosopher suggests that human life in its most human dimension is like a work of fiction, that man is a sort of novelist of himself, who conceives the fanciful figure of a personage with its unreal occupations and then, for the sake of converting it into reality, does all the things he does. Lowry says this idea recommends itself to him because he feels that man is a kind of novelist of himself. He thinks, too, that there is something valuable from a philosophic point of view in trying to put down what actually takes place in a novelist's mind when he conceives what he conceives to be the fanciful figure of a personage.

The part that never gets written, with which are included the true impulses that made him a novelist or dramatist in the first place, and the modifications of life around him through his own eyes as those impulses were realized, would be the true drama, and I hope to finish something of this sort one day.

At this point he inserts a long parenthesis in minute handwriting in the margin of his typed letter, which I quote in full, because its remarks on Pirandello exhibit the honesty, fairness and insight of his literary criticism:

> This would be not unlike Pirandello who — I quote from an article in *The Partisan Review*—"inverts the convention of modern realism, instead of pretending that the stage is not a stage at all, but the familiar parlour, he pretends that the familiar parlour is not real as a photograph *but a stage* containing many realities." This is Shakespeare's speech come true. My feeling is that Pirandello may not have wholly appreciated how close to truth his view of human life might be, as a consequence of which the realities of "Six Characters in Search of an Author," say, do not measure up to the profundity of the view, though I have not studied him sufficiently, and the accepted critical opinion upon Pirandello is apparently faulty.

Lowry continues his analysis of Ortega's *Towards a Philosophy of History* by stating that although Ortega is not concerned in this work, at any rate, with fiction, it is the thesis upon which he bases his view of history — namely, that man is what has happened to him. This thought interests Lowry because it is a philosophy that begins with one's existence, links up with Heidegger and Kierkegaard, and hence with Existentialism. Writing in June, 1950, he notes that Existentialism has already become a music hall joke in France and that it contains an element of despair that is absent in Ortega. Sartre's Existentialism, as far as he can understand it, strikes him as "a sort of reach-me-down or second-hand philosophy", changed dramatically to fit the anguish of the French in their struggle against the German occupation. In conclusion, however, he says:

> Even so, it is refreshing to read a philosophy that gives value to the drama of life itself, of the dramatic value of your own life at the very moment you are reading.

Commenting on Ortega's thought that the snob is hostile to liberalism, with the hostility of a deaf man for words, that liberty has always been understood in Europe as the freedom to be one's real self and that it is not surprising that a man who knows that he has no mission to fulfil should want to be rid of it, Lowry says that this idea at first sight appeared to him, among other things, one of the most convincing arguments against communism that he had ever read in such a short space, but that on second thought he realized it was only a statement in defence of the old school of liberalism, and he states that such a school could not exist without the possibility of free discussion of revolutionary tenets, including even those contained in communism for that matter, or without the right to practical absorption of revolutionary tenets where desirable.

THE POLITICAL SITUATION in the world looked grim to Lowry in 1950, although it did not seem to him half so hopeless as it had done in 1939 or even in 1938. In one letter, for instance, he writes: "Sometimes I get the impression that not even the people who are actually in the process of making history know in the least what is *really* going on. Or if they do, it seems appalling that they should be in the position that they are." As for the eventual outcome of the present human predicament, he felt that mankind, striving toward a rebirth, would probably achieve a better world in the not too-distant future. He was familiar, of course, with the pessimistic picture drawn by Orwell in his *1984*, as he often talked about the novel; but he was more hopeful than Orwell, and although he was painfully aware that man, if he did not take care, might destroy himself — as we might infer from *Under the Volcano* — he felt that the revolutionary forces of our time would change for the better the present shocking situation in world politics. He says, optimistically, that "anything that is a revolution must keep moving or it doesn't revolute: by its nature it contains within it the seeds of its own destruction; so by 1989, say, everything ought to be hunky-dory, all of which certainly doesn't make it any easier to live in 1950."

Elsewhere Lowry discusses at length religion, witchcraft and Voodooism — subjects in which he took an intense interest. Referring to *Mythologie Vodou*, a book on witchcraft, by his Haitian friend, Milo Marcelin, he takes exception to a review of it in *Time* magazine; he explains that it is a book not about Voodoo chiefly but about witchcraft, and that there is a difference, although it is not perhaps apparent to the layman.

Lowry points out that Voodoo is essentially a religion to be regarded with reverence, since it is without question a matter-transcending religion based upon the actual existence of the supernatural — a fact that is fundamental to man himself, compared with which most other religions are simply techniques to hide that fact or at least to keep the supernatural at relatively safe distances. He feels that only the Negroes are powerful enough or holy enough to be able to handle it, and that even they of course abuse it. He thinks, furthermore, that the white man should regard with awe the great dignity and discipline that is behind Voodooism at its highest, its conception of God and the meaning it gives to life — and this he says is the religion of a race that we so often glibly think of as inferior, or comprising medicine men, or the powers of darkness, etc. He appeals for greater understanding of the coloured people with words that are as timely today as when he wrote them ten years ago:

> Heart of Darkness indeed! Joseph Conrad should have been to Haiti. What he failed to understand was that the savages of the Congo had, to some extent, *subdued* the dark forces that are in nature by creating their religion in the first place in order to subdue them, that that, in its way, was a civilizing, almost a pragmatic process ... It is clear that Comrade Joseph did not allow himself to be corrupted by any savages though; he stayed in Polish aloofness on board in company with some *a priori* ideas.

Lowry himself felt that in his rich and varied life there had been many communications between his mind and others by means outside the channels of sense, and he was so convinced of the existence of thought transference that he could not dismiss it as mere coincidence. The subject of telepathy occurs often in his letters. Once a "mysterious" crossing of our letters (this resulted in much confusion and the resort to telegrams) caused him to write:

> I am being so supermeticulous about what is more or less spontaneous because I perceive, having been reading *Bergson*, that the difficulties on one plane of communication and the too great facilities on another (if telepathic ones can be called such), might have led you into some inconvenience, than which little is worse on Saturday afternoon ...

MALCOLM LOWRY was blessed with a keen sense of humour, though critics seem to have overlooked this priceless quality in his writings. He once said that he intended to write a book dealing with the peculiar punishment that is meted out to people who lack the sense of humour to write books like *Under the Volcano*. He was, in fact, a very witty person, and his wit could not help overflowing into his letters. It usually appears in a tone of good-natured banter. Commenting on the reception *Under the Volcano* received in France, he writes facetiously:

> Finally, I thought that you would be tickled to know, *The Volcano* has made a hit in France, where it is coming out three times in the next month: first in a classic series, then *Correa*, and it is also being serialized in the Paris daily news-

paper, *Combat*. They have decided that it is the writing on the wall, that your amigo is everything from the *Four Quartets* (which he has never read) to Joyce (whom he dislikes)—finally relate him to the Jewish prophetic Zohar (of which he knows nothing)—they have some other comments, too, about Macbeth, but that is nothing to what someone is just going to say in Victoria, over the C.B.C., where they have decided that the Consul is really Moby Dick, masquerading as the unconscious aspect of the Cadborosaurus in the Book of Jonah, or words to that effect.

A knowledgeable devotee of the cinematographic art, Lowry once said that if *Under the Volcano* were filmed in his lifetime, he would insist on helping to direct it, and in his letters he makes many interesting references to films. He tells, for instance, of going to see the film *The Hairy Ape*, which he had heard was good; he considered it *djevelsk* (Scandinavian for devilish) in the worst sense, although the suspense was subtly increased by the accident of the lights failing for an hour right in the middle of the showing. He recalls that people looked very sinister and strange standing about in the foyer, and he made a note that he ought to use this in a book; then he remembered that he had done so in *Under the Volcano*. In another letter he says that he went to see the old silent film *Intolerance*, played straight through without any music at all, which he considered a great mistake, as Griffith wrote his own score. "Very few silent films," he remarks, "will stand being played like that, without music, which I think is interesting. *The Passion of Joan of Arc* is an exception."

With regard to C. F. Ramuz's novel, *When the Mountain Fell*, Lowry makes some enlightening remarks on the author's style, in which he detects the influence of the movies. From his reading of Clifton Fadiman's remarks printed on the cover of *When the Mountain Fell*, he had gained the impression that Ramuz's style was being approached in an odd way, that it was supposed to be natural — that is, artless, unsophisticated, stark, stern, unintellectual, above all uninfluenced. He says he cannot see how a style, no matter how arrived at — often he imagines largely by cutting — can hope fundamentally to be much more than simply appropriate, in the fullest sense, to what the author is writing about. He says also that he did not find Ramuz's style particularly simple and that he can detect many sophisticated influences including avant-garde cinema. But as far as he is concerned the story is none the worse for that. His concluding remarks on style are illuminating:

> Just the same one is all in favour of a clear, pure, concrete style, and one with the utmost of simplicity, etc. But if one has arrived at that position, it is unlikely

that the style has been uninfluenced. Doubtless one has to pass through a maximum of influences before achieving a style at all. It is difficult to see how a style like Ramuz, even if it achieves great clarity, can be called unsophisticated. Anyhow his simplicity, such as it is, strikes me as having cost a great intellectual effort.

Lowry's life-long interest in style, as well as his deep love of language and his ready championship of the outcast, mark him as a kindred spirit of the great Austrian critic and poet Karl Kraus, who, like Lowry, concerned himself throughout his life with literary style and poetics, carried on an unending campaign against inaccurate and slovenly use of language, and fought against injustice, corruption and hypocrisy wherever he found them. Lowry doubtless knew the work of Kraus, because he was steeped in the writings of the authors of Central Europe. He often spoke in admiration of Kraus's compatriot and contemporary — Hermann Broch. But he talked most about the German-Jewish novelist, Franz Kafka, who like himself was definitely influenced by the Cabbala and the works of Sören Kierkegaard. There is much of Kafka's philosophical and religious symbolism — as well as traces of his compact, intense and closely reasoned style — in *Under the Volcano*. In his conversations Lowry made frequent references to *The Trial* and *The Castle*, and in one letter he writes that he appreciates a Kafka-like scrupulousness on my part, but hastens to remind me that "Kafka believed that while the demand on the part of the divine powers for absolute righteousness even in the smallest matters was unconditional, human effort, even at its highest, was always in the wrong."

Lowry had great sympathy for the younger authors who were struggling for recognition and was most generous in assisting them. When he reviewed their work, he made his criticism in the spirit of kindness, but he could be caustic, as when he reviewed Thomas Merton's *The Seven Story Mountain*. He considered it a very questionable book — a paradox, in fact; for Merton had gone into a Trappist monastery pretending to give up *everything* and yet went on writing books. But even in Merton's book Lowry recognized a kind of sincerity or dedication and felt that the book was important enough at this point in history to be considered on another plane altogether. He ends his entertaining review with a timely, striking thought: "That a Monastery *might*, in essence, be the capital of the world at this juncture is a possibility which not even Nietzsche were he alive would care to question — or would he?"

No account of Malcolm Lowry's life and work at Dollarton could be complete without mention of his love of British Columbia and especially the country closely surrounding his shack on Burrard Inlet. His descriptions of it permeate his fiction and the abundance of feeling he had for the place overflows into his letters. The fear that he might be evicted from his beloved house on the beach caused him much anxiety which he expresses in his letters. Nor did these feelings end on his departing to Europe in 1954. From Ripe, near Lewes, in Sussex, he wrote in April, 1956: "Though we like this place quite a bit, please don't think we have abandoned Dollarton; we have not and think of it constantly." And finally, about seven months before his untimely death, he wrote these nostalgic words: "I am writing like mad on *October Ferry to Gabriola* ... It is better than the *Volcano*, a veritable symphony of longing for the beach. We hope to return D.V., meantime think of you often and are often homesick."

Reading Lowry's letters again was a great pleasure for me. The immense vitality, the exuberant humour, the depth of thought and the broad humanity expressed on almost every page, often in the richest of poetic imagery, gave me moments of sheer delight. As a tribute to Malcolm Lowry — the man and the artist, I should like to quote, in closing, from a poem of his friend, Conrad Aiken, for whom he had the greatest admiration and who in turn cherished him as if he were his own son:

> Music I heard with you was more than music,
> And bread I broke with you was more than bread.

(1961)

LOWRY'S READING

W. H. New

IN TWO LARGE BOXES at the University of British Columbia are the remnants of Malcolm Lowry's library, a motley collection of works that ranges from Emily Brontë and Olive Schreiner to Djuna Barnes and Virginia Woolf, from the *Kenyon, Partisan,* and *Sewanee Reviews* to *A Pocketful of Canada,* from *Latin Prose Composition* to the *Metropolitan Opera Guide,* and from Elizabethan plays to Kafka and Keats. Little escaped his attention, in other words, and even such a partial list as this one indicates his eclectic and energetic insatiability for books. That he was also an inveterate film-goer and jazz enthusiast, and that he absorbed and remembered everything he experienced, makes any effort to separate out the individual influences on his work an invidious one; rather like chasing a rabbit through Ali Baba's caves, the activity seems incommensurate with its surroundings. But on frequent occasions an appreciation of the scope of his references or the source of a single allusion will take us closer to Lowry's tone and method.

Richard Hauer Costa, for example, writing in the *University of Toronto Quarterly* in 1967, points out that "unacknowledged literary kinship" between *Under the Volcano,* Aiken's *Blue Voyage,* and Joyce's *Ulysses*: the central use of the quest theme, the burgeoning sense of remorse, the "impatience" of the author with usual narrative methods, and so on. The Consul's "garden scene" in Chapter Five thus becomes an analogue to Joyce's Nighttown episode, and Lowry's dislocation of time, his recognition of what Costa elsewhere calls the "weight of the past", relates to Joyce's and Proust's. Such parallels have their value. It is by comparison that we learn our way into a new novel, and only after this process has taken place that we come to understand the individuality (if it exists) of the novel's own world.

Lowry acknowledges the comparative approach when in 1951 he finds in the work of Hermann Hesse the closest spirit to his own. And Clifford Leech uses comparison as a technical method in *Imagined Worlds* (1968) when, to investigate the "free manipulation of event" that characterizes the structure of Conrad's *Nostromo*, he brings in an analysis of *Under the Volcano* to illuminate his discussion. In both books the simultaneity of present and past, achieved by allowing an equivocal double viewpoint of character and narrator, affects our understanding of the situations and the ideas. As Leech puts it: "to have lived and to be the subject of anguish in recollection is in some sense to be living still." This has one meaning with reference to the Consul and Laruelle, another with reference to Lowry. On a still larger scale the statement could apply as one of the aims of criticism, or one of the accomplishments of art — to recreate the moment (of anguish, terror, hope, or whatever) that the author wished to convey, or to continue to engender that experience as the moment (and so the reader) alters; but these are aspects of the same problem of freedom and fate, essentially metaphysical in nature, which all of Lowry's work continually explores.

Lowry envisioned the universe as a series of Chinese boxes, with man in one of them, controlling some and controlled by others. The scheme is not quite so simple, of course, for the boxes (both external and internal) can be "factual" in any number of epistemological systems. And the whole prospect is further complicated by matters of fate and free will. Man can either control the worlds inside his mind or himself be governed, be in harmony with the sensory worlds outside him or be terrified and dislocated — and about such abstract possibilities as Destiny and Judgement (however tangible their effects in his life) he can only suppose. The scene in "Through the Panama", where Wilderness (aboard a ship in the Canal Zone) has relinquished control to the Captain, the Canal operator, and the Canal Zone Authority, is apropos. The overt image of multiple containment is obvious; embodied in it is a metaphor about the sensibility of an artist — not only to the materials that can be rendered into art but also to his own engagement with the task. The artist, that is, pursues control over a body of knowledge until it catches him and takes him over. Such knowledge is the "strange comfort" that the profession provides — whether it be the S.S. *Diderot*'s captain's extra ability and hence extra grounds for fear in the face of a strong storm, or Keats' medical knowledge disabusing his mind of any hope of recovery from his tuberculosis, or Sigbjørn Wilderness-cum-Malcolm Lowry's absorption in the present-ness of the past. The past cannot be escaped nor its reality (as preserved in memory, or in Wilderness's notebook, or in Lowry's novel) denied. Herein lies the thematic basis for both *Hear Us O Lord* and *Dark as the Grave*, and a further indication of the author's structural method.

In Lowry's letters we find other ramifications of this question of control. In 1951 he acknowledges Jung's concept of "man in search of a soul" as important to his work; in 1950 and again in 1953 Pirandello's *Six Characters in Search of an Author* suggests a "not dissimilar theme", which he relates to Existentialism and to Ortega's philosophy of history. Wilderness he identifies as "Ortega's fellow, making up his life as he goes along, and trying to find his vocation." "According to Ortega," moreover, "the best image for man himself *is* a novelist," being written by his books as much as writing them. In Lowry's case, any perception of events-in-time is complicated by his literary experience, so that Faust and the Castle of Udolpho and Dante *in purgatorio* start to have *in him* a reality equally as forceful as the "actual" direct influence of, say, Aiken and Dollarton and Nordahl Grieg. The references multiply: Poe's maelstrom can be stepped into, O'Neill's long day's journey can be followed into night, Fitzgerald's crackup can be experienced again in "Through the Panama", though it can end this time not in fission but in healing. Again the topics are pursued till they become his own: they cease to be *objects read* and become part of the subjectivity with which he renders experience.

A s DAVID BENHAM shows in his essay on *Lunar Caustic*, the presence of Herman Melville in Lowry's work provides another plane on which to approach questions of good and evil and the reality of the perceptions of the human mind. God and the devil — if not carrying all their Methodist connotations — do exert themselves in Lowry's world; heaven and hell exist. That one must descend to "hell" before locating "heaven" is a Jungian, Romantic concept he accepts completely — with the added implication that *in* the Inferno *is* Paradise, if we can see it. For Heriot in *Ultramarine*, Plantagenet in *Lunar Caustic*, and Wilderness in *Hear Us O Lord*, this is worked out in separate metaphors of voyage and discovery; for the consul it is tied up with his alcoholic descent into a Mexico that is both a landscape of fact and a state of mind. To be drunk is to be *in extremis* as far as the rational world is concerned, yet for the Consul it is paradoxically also a way of most vividly perceiving his own relationship with others. Seeing things clearly, still differs from acting on the basis of that perception. In her recent book, *The Private Labyrinth of Mal-*

colm Lowry (1969), for example, Perle Epstein has pointed out how the Consul's vision, for all its profundity and accuracy, is a sterile one because his talents are never exercised in an effort to grasp the harmony, the heaven, that (as for "successful" characters like Cosnahan or Wilderness) lay in his path.

The problem of harmonizing the mind with the outside environment is, of course, a central one in works like Coleridge's "Rime of the Ancient Mariner", which Lowry absorbed so thoroughly as to bind it integrally into the structure and effect of "Through the Panama". From Coleridge, Lowry also accepted many of his ideas about the fluidity of time — a more direct borrowing, in fact, than anything from Joyce or Proust. Yet Coleridge himself absorbed so much — from the occult sciences and elsewhere — and influenced so many, that the question of primary and secondary routes of influence seems a tangle too dense to uncoil. Much came via Nordahl Grieg, for example, whom Lowry met in 1930; much came via J. W. Dunne's *An Experiment with Time* (1927), a book examining the proposition that the future can be objectively experienced in the past. Though it had a strong following during the decade or so after its publication, it has also been attacked — for "spatializing" a non-spatial concept, for identifying the problems of time passing with those of time passed, and for interpreting time as itself a process in time — but such objections did not particularly disturb Lowry. Paul Tiessen shows how Lowry's "cinematic" technique in works like *Under the Volcano*, for example, is adapted to presenting temporal flux in spatial terms. *Dark as the Grave* extends the method and most clearly demonstrates Dunne's idea.

Whereas Dunne may prove finally unacceptable to philosophical theoreticians, Lowry perceived the applicability of the theory to the process by which an artist attaches himself to his work and then is separated from it. His novel *Dark as the Grave*, that is, concerns his character Wilderness (another novelist) discovering the separation between himself and his own character Trumbaugh — in a linear sequence that opens up Dunne's notion of "regress": events in time past, relived in the memory, occur simultaneously in time present, which epitomizes in its way the process of "re-creation" that reading a novel involves readers in. But further: Wilderness, returning to his own and his novel's Mexican past, is still moving through time into the future. Out of his memory of the past he anticipates events in the future, which possess a vivid and objective reality for him and do "happen". On the basis of this "dream" experience, however, the will may exert itself and thus alter the nature of the "actual" experience that subsequently occurs. To Lowry this process was extremely important. Certain as he was that there existed a unity between life and death, body and soul, reality and unreality, he found here a key to the metaphysics that joined them.

His search in Kant's *Critique of Pure Reason* was for answers to one of the dilemmas he found himself in, and his passion for fateful coincidences led him into the works of P. D. Ouspensky (*A New Model of the Universe*, 1931) and Charles Fort (particularly *Lo!*, 1931; *Wild Talents*, 1932; and *The Book of the Damned*, 1919). He travelled to Haiti (in 1947) to discover something about Voodoo, and become interested there in the work of a young Haitian writer named Philippe Thoby-Marcelin. He found occult signs in the natural world about him, and in order to interpret them, as Geoffrey Durrant suggests, he seems to have absorbed many of the ideas of Neoplatonism that developed from the school of Porphyry. Even his interest in the Greek Classics stems from this search for omens and explanations; throughout *Ultramarine* the Eumenides sound their voices, for example, till Hilliot hears. And in the later work — particularly the manuscript pages of *October Ferry to Gabriola* and *La Mordida* — fragments from Ouspensky, Tourneur, Plato, Fort, and the *I Ching* are gathered together to influence and explain the fate of Ethan and Jacqueline Llewelyn and of Sigbjørn and Primrose Wilderness.

But if Lowry sympathized with the pursuits of Ouspensky and Fort, it is in the work of a Vancouver Cabbalist named Charles Robert Stansfeld-Jones ("Frater Achad") — an acquaintance of the better known English mystic Aleister Crowley — that he found much of the occult *system* on which some of his later writing hangs. Jones's work — particularly *Q.B.L., or the Bride's Reception* and *The Anatomy of the Body of God*, privately published during the 1920's — explores the theory that the universe is constantly expanding yet constantly ordered. In his terms, the expansion can be seen in the psychic progress of adepts within it; the order is described by the principles and symbols of Cabbala, which will allow to an adept the knowledge that can lead to hell or to heaven, to the barranca or the garden, to torment or to peace. Thus numbers, colours, animals, and all the symbols of the Tarot pack acquire a meaning that is significant not only within the framework of an individual story but also within the constructs of occult philosophy.

Lowry's unpublished fragment *The Ordeal of Sigbjørn Wilderness* (like *Lunar Caustic* set in a hospital) makes the metaphysical intent of human "ordeal" quite explicit; an authorial note quotes from the Anglo-Irish theosophist Annie Besant to explain the several kinds of spiritual truth in religion:

(1) One eternal infinite incognizable real Existence.

(2) From THAT the manifested God, unfolding from unity to duality, from duality to trinity.

(3) From the manifested Trinity many spiritual intelligences, guiding the Kosmic order.

(4) Man a reflection of the manifested God and therefore a trinity fundamentally, his inner and real self being eternal, one with the Self of the universe.

(5) His evolution by repeated incarnations, into which he is drawn by desire, and from which he is set free by knowledge and sacrifice, becoming divine in potency as he had ever been divine in latency.

The passage explains much of what Lowry intended by the multiple identities that Wilderness possesses and much of the thematic unity that he hoped to develop by joining all his works into a single cycle to be called *The Voyage that Never Ends*. In that context the fiction repudiates the more obvious platitudes about character and plot analysis, and transcends even the basic structure Lowry admits to deriving from the *Divine Comedy*, in order to try to render all human experience and all its paradoxes of time, place, and perception, in something more emotionally overwhelming than abstract terms. Possibly for that reason the task was not completed; because of Lowry's own developing understanding, it never could be.

Not all of the influences that impinged on Lowry's consciousness can be as precisely dated as that of Charles Jones, who arrived in Lowry's life as a census enumerator in 1941. He was frequently provided with cogent subplots and evocative images, for example — as can be seen in *Under the Volcano*, or the published chapter from *October Ferry*, or the manuscript pages of a story like "Ghostkeeper" — by reading such ephemeral material as neighbourhood newspapers. His knowledge of the Greek and Roman Classics, Shakespeare, and Dante, however, presumably dates from his English public school education; Aiken, Grieg, and jazz were undergraduate enthusiasms; John Davenport was a school acquaintance, and James Stern a friend from his Paris days in the early 1930's. But Lowry's casual references to Donne, Dostoevsky, Chatterton, Crabbe, Roethke, Chekhov, Faulkner, Farrell, Dylan Thomas, Ellison, Yeats and a host of others are dropped like handkerchiefs through his letters.

They have their pertinence and their own claims to recognition, but if we stop to pick them all up we run the the danger of being lured into aimless alleys.

Certainly many of the references to Canadian writing fall into this "blind" category. Lowry knew the work of Ralph Gustafson and Al Purdy and a pro-letarian poet of the early 1950's named Curt Lang — but not well, and not to the point of its affecting his own work in any observable way. It was really land-scape more than culture that influenced him in Canada. One particularly pointed passage in *October Ferry* makes this clear: if Canada has any originality at all it lies in its uncontrolled wilderness. To be taming it is one thing; to have it tamed is another — a dead situation that demands undoing in order to begin afresh. So the physical environment furnished him once again with a metaphor for the artist's predicament: to be taming the wilderness of language and ideas is more exhilarating than to have accomplished the task. To know that and yet still to be spurred into writing created an ironic dilemma that was Lowry's own.

He did know some writers in Canada, like Dorothy Livesay and Earle Birney, better than Gustafson and Lang, and in *Turvey* he found an ironic sensibility towards society to match his own. It is an important point, for it forces us to recognize the neglected but obvious truth that Lowry's work is genuinely comic. In all his grim systematizing there is room for laughter, and his observation of "Joyce's complaint re *Ulysses*: 'They might at least have said it was damned funny' ", has a kind of reflexive barb attached to it. Perhaps this is simply another way of showing how heaven is linked with hell — or how, as in "Elephant and Colosseum", man's reaching for harmony is linked with his perception of "God's joke": the elephant. For the joke has its serious side; the elephant is named Rosemary, and "remembrance" (as *October Ferry* and *Dark as the Grave* remind us) can work both as escape from the present and as conscience to remind us of the "normality" of guilt — another example of the "strange comfort" that the fact of being human affords to an individual man.

Such a process of "taming" his own landscapes led to his constant revision of his work, his constant search for knowledge, his continual urge to read more and to begin writing again. Early in 1949 (while *Turvey* was being written), Lowry wrote to Birney to express his delight in the book. After discovering its seriousness as well as its comedy, and likening it to *The Good Soldier Schweik* and *Dangling Man* and *Dead Souls*, he adds a significant note on Gogol:

The swing between farce and the purely lyrical might be of value technically. And the almost Moussorgsky-like sadness and longing he is able to distil simply by describing some crummy little hotel.

The range and apparent casualness of the references is typical; the fragmentariness of the observation suggests a characteristic process of authorial note-taking, both for Wilderness and himself. Like other references to his reading, it shows not only the importance he attached to the things he encountered, but also the metamorphosis they underwent in his mind. At the same time, it offers us a glimpse of his ideas in the process of being born.

(1970)

MALCOLM LOWRY
AND THE CINEMA

Paul G. Tiessen

Lowry's thorough knowledge and appreciation of cinematic technique came from his sustained, intense interest in the world of the film, a world in which he participated as viewer, critic and writer. His own words express best his ardent enthusiasm as a viewer, even while he was living outside the urban area of Vancouver:

> I think I have seen nearly all the great German films, since the days of *Caligari*, some of them many times, risking my neck even when at school (where movies were forbidden) to see . . . Conrad Veidt in *The Student of Prague*, and Murnau's wonderful things, all the films of the great Ufa days, and other later masterpieces. . . . and it is an enthusiasm that has not deserted me, for only recently we [Lowry and his wife Margerie] have trekked through the snow, (still risking our necks — physically on these occasions because of the ice) just to keep up with the times, to see Murnau's *Last Laugh*, Fritz Lang's *Destiny* (a pioneer piece if there ever was one) and other contemporary films and Klangfilms at the local Vancouver Film Society.[1]

This exuberant reaction to the great German films had already been expressed in Chapter One of *Under the Volcano*, where M. Laruelle, a former film director, nostalgically recalling his past, reflects Lowry's personal interest in

> the old days of the cinema. . . . his own delayed student days, the days of the *Student of Prague*, and Wiene and Werner Krauss and Karl Gruene, the Ufa days when a defeated Germany was winning the respect of the cultured world by the pictures she was making.

The life-long relationship between Lowry and the cinema reveals itself everywhere in his work. Lowry himself was not unaware of the pervasive influence of the cinema, particularly that of Germany, upon his own work:

> Nor has anything I have read influenced my own writing personally more than the first twenty minutes of Murnau's *Sonnenaufgang* or the first and the last shots of Kark Gruene's *The Street*.[2]

133

As film-writer, Lowry first spent an unhappy period of time working in Hollywood, shortly before beginning his original short-story version of *Under the Volcano* in 1936:

> He worked on several movie scripts, with John [Davenport], a friend from Cambridge days and others. He was always interested in the cinema . . . but he was unhappy in Hollywood; he didn't like their methods of working, or much of their results, and he found it difficult to work in tandem with several other writers on the same script. So as soon as possible he left Hollywood and went to Mexico.[3]

In a comment referring to *Las Manos de Orlac*, the film which is of symbolic significance in his novel, *Under the Volcano*, Lowry's mock-praise of Hollywood's version of that movie — "a remake . . . of truly awe-inspiring badness"[4] — wryly records his reaction to the American movie factory. However, the Hollywood experience did provide Lowry with the opportunity of becoming directly involved in the practical application of cinema technique. Later, his work — particularly his two unpublished screen scripts and his main novel — was to provide evidence of his interests in and experience with the cinema.

One of the two unpublished film scripts, "The Bravest Boat", is a delicate screen adaptation of his own beautifully and sensitively woven short-story of the same title. However, his much more significant contribution to film art — "by no means an ordinary kind of script"[5] — is his "Tender is the Night", a 455-page movie version of F. Scott Fitzgerald's novel. Lowry worked on this great cinema-piece in 1949 and 1950 in collaboration with his wife Margerie. Frank Taylor's assessment of the work is certainly valid. In a letter to Lowry he observed:

> I have read many scripts and seen many pictures, but never before have I seen writing so purely cinematic. The impact of your work was much, much greater than that of the novel. It goes devastatingly deep, and its direct filmic evocation of life's complexities is magic and miraculous.[6]

In his arrangement of concrete visual images chosen specifically for the camera-eye, Lowry employs many devices analogous to those which he uses in his novel, *Under the Volcano*. Thus, the critical commentary which Lowry interspersed throughout the massive manuscript expands the reader's understanding of Lowry's techniques not only in the film-script but also in his novel.

A few years after the publication of *Under the Volcano*, Lowry considered the possibility of doing a screen adaptation of the novel. His insistence that it be done in Germany was his greatest personal compliment to the film art of that country:

Nothing could make us happier — happy is not the word, in fact — and what an opportunity it is! — than for a film to be made of the *Volcano* in Germany, providing it were done in the best tradition of your great films.[7]

In typically buoyant letter-writing style, Lowry modestly recommends himself and his wife as writers who might be exceptionally eligible for such an undertaking:

I would myself very much wish to make a treatment of the *Volcano* for the film, and I would be very anxious to work on that and the scenario with my wife, who not only was a movie actress for years, but has collaborated on one film with me ... and who ... knows the *Volcano* backwards ... : so, incidentally do I, though I say it myself, and we are a first class team, the like of which is scarcely to be found, I dare say, even in Germany or anywhere else....[8]

Even though Lowry did not write the projected scenario, the cinematic idiom which he had already used in the novel would have made the problem of transposition relatively simple.

In ANY CINEMATIC SCRIPT the role played by the concrete pictorial images is of primary concern. The camera itself is used to write the visual poetry. Other elements take their cue from the visual image. In *Under the Volcano*, to make the reader consciously aware of the primary role of visual idiom in the work, Lowry intermittently draws attention by implication or direct reference to the nature of the camera itself as a medium of perception.

During the bus-ride of chapter eight, for example, the bus's windows mechanically define the margins of the scene outside the bus, as if the "movement" of the countryside and the volcano is being held within the margins of a rectangular movie screen. A quick visual rhythm is created by the ominous recurrence of the changing shapes of the volcano. Long-shots alternate with close-ups:

As, descending, they circled round and round, Popocatepetl slid in and out of view continually, never appearing the same twice, now far away, then vastly near at hand, incalculably distant at one moment, at the next looming round the corner....

The circular movement of the bus imitates the panning motion of a mobilized motion picture camera. The successively alternating views of the central space-object, the volcano, provides an effect analogous to that produced by film montage, in which "discontinuous" visual fragments of spatial reality are edited and juxtaposed.

135

As the novel proceeds and the Consul literally moves closer and closer to the threatening form of the volcano and to death, a much heavier visual rhythm is established by the insistently regular, temporal reappearance of Popocatepetl, of whose nearing presence the reader is constantly kept aware. First the volcano is reflected within the frame of Yvonne's mirror which, again mimicking movie-making apparatus, mechanically manipulates her view so that she sees only the one volcano. Popocatepetl now was "nearer, looking over her shoulder. . . . [But] however she moved the mirror she couldn't get poor Ixta in." Thus, mechanical devices preclude the visual reunion of the legendary lovers, Ixta and Popocatepetl. Some time later, as the Consul cries, "I love hell," and (rejecting life with Yvonne) flees toward death in the *barranca*, it seems as if a camera is shooting a close-up to emphasize the fact that his destruction is already upon him:

> Before him the volcanoes, precipitous, seemed to have drawn nearer. They towered up over the jungle, into the lowering sky — massive interests moving up in the background.

The seething rhythm, beating out the rushing approach of inevitable death, does not cease; and several pages later another, closer shot, taken at a sharp angle, imposes itself upon the eye of the reader's imagination:

> . . . the whole precipitous bulk of Popocatepetl seemed to be coming towards them . . . leaning forward over the valley.

Finally the intense visual rhythm stops. It strikes its final resounding note above the head of the Consul, who is being meagrely sustained in the end by nothing but two death-laden mescals:

> Popocatepetl towered through the window, its immense flanks partly hidden by rolling thunderheads; its peak blocking the sky, it appeared almost right overhead, [the Consul] directly beneath it. Under the volcano!

The immense mass of the volcano spreads across the screen, which is here defined by the window of the bar. That a static landscape has been imbued with a sense of flux in which temporal form is given to the visual death-rhythm of the volcano is essentially cinematic. "In the cinema," it has been said, "space loses its static quality and acquires a time-charged dynamic quality. Parts of space are arranged in a temporal order and become part of a temporal structure with a temporal rhythm."[9]

The first four paragraphs of *Under the Volcano* demonstrate a method of introduction which also is analogous to a traditionally conventional camera technique in the film medium itself: the camera varies its range from long-shots to close-ups, from the universal to the intimate. Indeed, this is the method which Lowry uses in his two film scripts as well. To introduce "Tender is the Night":

> The picture opens in dead silence with a tremendous shot of the night sky, the stars blazing. . . .
>
> The camera seems to be bearing down upon us, so that the sensation we have is of receding downwards from the sky and the moon, and from this rhythm to the earth.
>
> The next instant the clouds become smoke coming out of a tunnel from which we see a train emerging into morning sunlight; the next we are in this train . . . with Rosemary Hoyt and her mother, watching the landscape of the French Riviera out of the window. Immediately we draw almost to a stop before a sign standing in a field. . . .
>
> Meantime, as the camera comes closer, we see as much as is necessary . . . of the sign itself. . . :
>
> Touriste Americaine! Vous vous approchez maintenant de la ville ancienne d'ANTIBES. . . . Everything for the American tourist at popular prices!

The cheap commercial seediness here emphasized by the final close-up contrasts with an overwhelming sense of awe inspired by the initial long-shot.

In Lowry's first paragraph of the film script, "The Bravest Boat", the relationship between the camera movement there — from long-shot to close-up — and that of *Under the Volcano* is at once self-evident:

> In long shot we see the rip-teeth of the winter-white mountains across the bay; closer in, the combers riding in toward shore; and close-up, what was there all along: the single flare of a rain-drenched blossom on a flowering tree. . . .

In *Under the Volcano*, first Mexico — associated by latitude with Hawaii and India — is the subject for the camera's bird's-eye view; for in Mexico Lowry has found a visual image for the expression of universal truth. Then the camera seems to zero in first on the whole town, Quauhnahuac, and then on the Hotel Casino de la Selva. Finally, a close-up of two men in white flannels introduces the reader particularly to M. Laruelle, the former film-producer, who will present to the reader a "re-run" of the story of death which took place one year before.

Another cinematic technique, one which the cinema may, in fact, have borrowed from literary art, is the mechanical use of typographical details which function with the same visual directness whether caught by a movie camera and reflected on a screen or whether figuratively caught by a camera and typographically reproduced on the pages of the novel. For example, the reader's visual sense is literally stimulated near the end of chapter eleven by the pictorial reproduction of the black hand, ominously confirming the direction of the Consul's plunge toward death. An extension of such visual, typographical detail is Lowry's use of foreign phrases or the words from posters, advertisements, postcards and newspaper headlines — always ironically informative, never thematically incongruous or artistically irritating. Speaking critically of a similar use of "signs, words, advertisements" in "Tender is the Night" Lowry says:

> ...all contributes to what one might call the subconscious life of the movie itself, thereby rendering it the more organic. More than that, such attention to detail, philosophically speaking, gives the film a sort of solipsistic world of its own which, if expressed in accordance with strict realism that in turn is in accordance with the actual historical facts, will inevitably increase our response to it by appealing to facets of the consciousness not usually called into play.... And since, finally, there have to be some signs, etc., why not, without overdoing it, some (as there are in life) significant ones?

In *Under the Volcano*, the choice of signs by the camera-eye, as it were, also provides visual landmarks which recurrently draw attention to the deep, spiritual currents of the novel.

Finally, concrete, visual images are used to create montage. Because the novel moves across a landscape of pictorial imagery which is depictable in terms of camera-perception, Lowry is provided with material to follow, at least in the figurative sense, Eisenstein's dictum: "Cinematography is, first and foremost, montage.... By the combination of two 'depictables' is achieved the representation of something that is graphically undepictable."[10] Throughout *Under the Volcano*, Lowry's subtle combination of a multiplicity of visual images creates a complexity of montage "explosions". Because visual details which are repeatedly associated with particular characters or occurrences in the novel are frequently juxtaposed by Lowry's camera-eye, the montage, by translating the themes of the novel into cinematic idiom, contributes to the tightly integrated structure of the novel. Deriving visual, emotional and conceptual depth from all aspects of the novel with which the visual image or image-clusters are associated, the montage in turn dynamically confers dimensions of increased significance to those parts. Frequently, for example, the conjunction of visual images exposes the tension of the emotional undercurrents which prevent real union and fellowship among the characters of the novel. The montage, in such instances, is an instrument of irony. The juxtaposed images are brought into contrast with the hypocritical, surface-dialogue which attempts to realize at least an illusion of propriety and brotherhood. For example, in chapter four, while the Consul sleeps, Hugh, his half-brother, who has already once betrayed the Consul by seducing Yvonne, persuades Yvonne to ride with him on horseback. As they move along, Lowry's camera-eye, selecting minute visual detail, informs the reader that "a lizard vanished into the bougainvillea growing along the road-bank, wild bougainvillea now, an overflux, followed by a second lizard." No explanation is required by the narrator. Nothing is spoken by Yvonne and Hugh. The "camera" alone, in its creation of montage while exploring the landscape, has graphically symbolized the passions beneath the decorous surface, as thoughts of adultery with Yvonne (bougainvillea) again creep into the mind of Hugh (lizard; reptile). Hugh's pictorial association with symbols of temptation and betrayal, with the "future-corruptive serpent," is graphically reinforced for the reader as "Hugh actually did ride over a garter-snake." In chapter five, upon waking, the Consul sees his wife and Hugh standing together, and he realizes that they have met once again while he was sleeping. "Yvonne's arms were full of bougain-villea. . . ;" and the Consul shouts to her companion, "Hi, there, Hugh, you old snake in the grass!" Vivid images of Yvonne, bougainvillea, Hugh and the serpent merge and explode to underline the unspoken fears and tensions lying beneath the surface of the dialogue.

Thus, Lowry selects, as the film-maker would, external objects which add dimension to the dialogue of his novel. Through the juxtapositioning of pictorial objects which, outside the context of his novel, would be emotionally "neutral," Lowry achieves a subtle means for expressing deepfelt, complex emotions. Indeed, in many instances, a rapid succession of externally depictable images provides Lowry with the best means for the surrealistic expression of the tormented inner world of the alcoholic. A vivid example of the combining of images to reveal the hallucinatory phantasmagoria of the inner world of the Consul also affects the reader's visual imagination: "the thin shadows of isolated nails, the stains of murdered mosquitoes, the very scars and cracks of the wall, had begun to swarm, so that, wherever he looked, another insect was born, wriggling instantly toward his heart."

In *Under the Volcano*, man has relegated the control of his own fate to the arbitrary relentlessness of inhuman forces. These forces, whether within man or external to man but created by him, come together in the image of the *máquina infernal*, the Infernal Machine. It is perhaps one of the most interesting aspects of Lowry's preoccupation with film technique that he uses images from the cinematic process itself — particularly the image of the motion picture reel, with its fragmented rendering of reality — to establish metaphors which will express the mechanized certainty of man's spiritual death.

The identification of the image of the motion picture reel with the image of other revolving wheels, particularly those of the Ferris wheel and the carrousel, is explicitly evident at several points in the novel. At the close of chapter one, for example, a movie reel in a forebodingly darkened room seems to transport the reader to a passage of time which has already begun and ended exactly one year before, and of which the ending is known to be death: "in the dark tempestuous night, backwards revolved the luminous wheel." Chapters two to twelve, unrolling like a strip of celluloid mechanically fixed with its immutable sequence of images, mercilessly record that death. Like the frequent use of flashbacks in the novel, these eleven chapters emphasize Lowry's anxious concern with time past. Thus, like the image of the motion picture reel, the form of the novel itself is circular, chapter one being both prologue and epilogue. Form merges with theme, then, as the pattern of inevitable death becomes tightly locked into the novel's spiral descent of soulless rotation. The mechanical circularity seems to preclude the admittance of love, trust, life. That the present cannot escape the past, that the impotence of man's present merges with the guilt of his past, is symbolically best expressed in a cinematic style where the circularity of the form, imitating the circular motion of the reel, can manipulate the overlapping and merging of time. Thus, while the novel, in Lowry's own words, must be accepted as "a prophecy, a political warning, a cryptogram, a crazy film, . . . [it also] can be thought of as a kind of machine."[11] The novel's rush downhill toward death unrolls with macabre and machine-like efficiency. Damnation is the only end. The blind, brutal wheel/reel of fortune, of fate, of time catches man on its circumference merely to crush him; just as the series of images on the celluloid strip permanently determines the course of the actor's — man's, Mexico's — jerky attempts to mimic life. Quite conscious of his own destruction, but too impotent to prevent it, man feels caught in "the spoked shadow of [a] wheel, enormous, insolent. . . ."

Lowry's graphic description of another attraction found at the midway further emphasizes his central preoccupation with the mechanized, circular image of the movie reel:

> The huge carrousel . . . was thronged by peculiar long-nosed wooden horses mounted on whorled pipes, dipping majestically as they revolved with a slow

piston-like circulation. . . . Jacques was pointing to the pictures on the panels running entirely around the inner wheel that was set horizontally and attached to the top of the central revolving pillar.

The construction and movement of this machine are remarkably similar to those of the innumerable forerunners of the modern movie reel itself. One such machine, for example, was simply a toy,

> . . . consisting of a peculiar circular receptable on a wooden stand. . . . You could tuck inside the rim [of the receptacle] . . . a series of small pictures depicting such images as a rider and horse jumping a fence. . . . In the centre of the receptacle was a [revolving] polygon of mirror faces. . . . If you kept your eyes fixed on only one of the faces of the mirror polygon, the riders appeared to jump.[12]

This toy, called a Praxinoscope, and many similar toys depending on the rotating circle for the effect of continuous movement and flux, inflexibly reiterated a mechanically predetermined illusion of life held within the futility of circular motion.

In chapter seven, still a third mechanical analogue to the movie reel provides Lowry with an image for the fullest and most vivid expression of a theme which involves the tyranny of the soulless machine. Here the Consul, who is now drunk and is trying hard to avoid involvement with the begging children who surround him, escapes confrontation with reality and life by merging himself literally with the blind reeling motion of the Infernal Machine. The Consul, who has lost all inner spirit of his own, crawls into the machine and, passively gives himself up to this "huge evil spirit, screaming in its lonely hell, its limbs writhing." Crowds watch passively too: it seems as if "no one could stop the machine, . . . the monster," which has taken control of the hapless man.

Thus, "trembling in every limb under [the] weight of the past," destitute, guilty man has acquiesced to the mechanized heartlessness of the machine, the wheel, the reel; and he has the feeling of being on the edge of a "drunken madly revolving world". But even the circular image of the motion picture reel — the novel's visual point of thematic reference — is but a parody of the organic unity and perfection usually associated with the circle. For while the celluloid, looping through the projector from the reel of the motion picture apparatus, attempts to affirm organic life and movement and flux, its unrolling can portray only a succession or series of static, inanimate, inorganic, fragmented still shots or frames. Each frame is separated by a dark temporal gap, a void, an abyss, a *barranca* — a "frightful cleft," where it is "too dark to see the bottom. . . . finality indeed, and cleavage!" As the *barranca*, or ravine, rending the Mexican landscape provides a concrete, visual image of the fragmentation of the community of man, so the separation between the frames provides a metaphor for disunity within mankind. Because this metaphor is also associated with the image of the motion picture reel, it reinforces the warning already implied by that image. The isolated, static frames of the mechanized monster, which man has set in motion and to which he has acquiesced, can provide only a lifeless travesty of real life; and in such a grip, man can "wait only for the ratification of death". He can wait only for the darkness, for the *barranca* between the frames, to swallow him up when his jerky movement ceases.

Just as Lowry draws attention to the image of the motion picture reel, he emphasizes the fragmentary quality of the film's attempts to reconstruct life. He stresses particularly the darkness of the temporal gap which precludes the possibility of organic life in the film. For example, the "illuminated news aloft travelling around the Times Building, . . . snapped off into darkness, into the end of a world. . . . And everywhere, that darkness, the darkness of a world without meaning, a world without aim." In another instance, the mutual isolation of each panel in the "procession of queer pictures" which circles the great carrousel emphasizes a mechanical fragmentation which apes life. Similarly, in his descriptions of a number of murals in *Under the Volcano*, Lowry stresses the disjointedness of each consecutive panel of the different murals. While the visual content of each mural brings into focus the themes of the novel, the medium itself suggests static fragmentation rather than organic life. In the *cantina* El Bosque, for example, a series of identical pictures illustrates a pack of wolves pursuing a sleigh "at intervals right round the room, though neither sleigh nor wolves budged an inch in the process." Here, not only the discontinuity between the pictures, but also the pictures themselves provide only static illusion of movement and life. Several such murals suggest the false impression of organic movement in film, where continuity is really being disintegrated by the darkness which interrupts the illusory persistence of light. Thus the machine which controls man is merely mimicking life while driving man toward death. Mechanically reiterated flashes of light, representing only superficial efforts to achieve organic unity, parallel man's superficial efforts to maintain the forms of brotherhood without love. The montage in the following example merges the theme, the technique and the controlling metaphor of the novel: "the lights of Quauhnahuac's one cinema . . . suddenly came on, flicked off, came on again. *'No se puede vivir sin amar'.*"

Unable to love, unable to accept love in a world full of social deception and mechanical guise, the Consul, in his drunken stupor, experiences more fully than all the other characters the finality and darkness and horrors of the *barranca* which keeps man lonely and alone. The metaphor of the *barranca*, while providing an analogue for the Consul's fragmented, uncontrolled perception, also points to the technique which Lowry uses. The flashback, with its dislocation of chronological time, and the camera-eye's juxtapositioning of disparate external objects to create montage, provide mechanical or stylistic parallels for the kind of incongruities which attract the Consul's attention. It seems as if a *barranca* slashes across his sense of sight to disintegrate its continuity into a "continual twitching and hopping within his field of vision," just as moments of darkness create the ultimate fragmentation of the motion picture.

Under the Volcano, then, is a coherent and integrated artistic expression of an incoherent and fragmented world. The images of the *barranca* and the wheel are of central importance. Both point to the synthesis of form and content at which Lowry arrives in the novel. There is a fusion of visual metaphor, theme, characterization and technique. The visual metaphors — wheels and *barranca* — draw much of their strength from their association with the cinematic process, in which mechanical fragmentation underlies the apparent continuity of the motion picture. In cinema technique, Lowry finds not only methods but also a metaphor to express the tormented, surrealistic world of his characters.

(1970)

FOOTNOTES

[1] Malcolm Lowry, unpublished letter, October 31, 1951; addressed to Herr Clenens ten Holder, German translator of *Under the Volcano*.

[2] *Ibid.*

[3] Margerie Lowry, "Malcolm Lowry's Life," unpublished biographical sketch.

[4] Malcolm Lowry, *Selected Letters of Malcolm Lowry*. Edited by Harvey Breit and Margerie Lowry (Philadelphia, 1965), 251.

[5] *Ibid.*, 309.

[6] Frank Taylor, *Selected Letters*, 441.

[7] Malcolm Lowry, unpublished letters, October 31, 1951.

[8] *Ibid.*

[9] Ralph Stephenson and J. R. Debrix, *The Cinema as Art* (Harmondsworth, 1967), 133.

[10] Sergei Eisenstein, *Film Form*, in *Film Form: Essays in Film Theory and The Film Sense*. Edited and translated by Jay Leyda (Cleveland and New York, 1967), 28, 30.

[11] Malcolm Lowry, "Preface to a Novel," translated from French to English by George Woodcock. *Canadian Literature*, IX (Summer, 1961). Clarisse Françillon's original French version, published in 1948, was based on Lowry's notes.

[12] Ivor Montagu. *Film World* (Harmondsworth, 1964), 18.

143

SWINGING
THE MAELSTROM

Malcolm Lowry and Jazz

Perle Epstein

W<small>HEN DURING THE COURSE</small> of treatment a psychiatrist
asked Malcolm Lowry to free associate "anything that comes into your head that
begins with *B*", Lowry instantly replied, "Bix Beiderbecke". For some reason
the psychiatrist would not accept this answer; if he had, he would have learned
a great deal about his patient in a short time. Had the therapist been a jazz
fan himself, he would have known that Beiderbecke, one of Lowry's lifetime
idols, played a brilliant trumpet and died an alcoholic at age twenty-eight. One
short step, and he would have understood that in many ways Bix was to jazz
what Lowry was to literature: an American counterpart (Bix was born in 1903,
Lowry in 1909), a restless student with a middle-class upbringing, an alcoholic,
a rebellious adolescent who left home to pursue an unconventional career, a
musician/nomad who was forever dissatisfied with his work. Both young men
had a propensity for seeking out father figures in their respective fields: Bix
found his mentor in Frank Trumbauer, a saxophone player who took the young
trumpeter under his wing, developed the young man's talent, and improved his
technique; Lowry's "literary father" was Conrad Aiken, who — as it is by now
well known — sheltered, fed, and unstintingly assisted the budding novelist.

Beiderbecke, the archetype for *Young Man With a Horn*, was an extremely
intelligent musician, a man familiar with literature who, after dipping into a
musical career at about the same age Lowry set out to sea, attempted to return
to college, but whose restless inability to cope with regulations and routine, drove
him away eighteen days after enrolling; here the young English amateur jazz
musician fared better (even during the darkest hours of his life, Lowry somehow

managed to draw Herculean draughts of discipline from some underground source) for he emerged from an unhappy stay at Cambridge with his classical tripos, armed and ready to write. Like Lowry too, it was at this age that Bix took up the drinking that was eventually to kill him.

Had the psychiatrist allowed his patient to free associate further, he might have learned that Lowry was an avid jazz fan as a youth at Cambridge, that he played the ukelele — or, as he called it, "taropatch" — described by Margerie Lowry as: "a long-range uke with more strings and frets, and that's what he played in later years though he started with a regular small ukelele", that he composed songs and worshipped Eddie Lang, a virtuoso jazz guitarist who, with his lifelong friend, violinist Joe Venuti, played with Beiderbecke and Trumbauer in the late twenties and early thirties. Lowry loved this essentially "white" sound of the classically trained jazzmen of the period — the controlled, formal tone of Bix Beiderbecke and the brilliant, driving rhythm of Lang. During the last few years of his life, however, Lowry's love for jazz abated; he decided to "leave it to the young" and turned his interest to classical music instead. But music, and especially jazz music, the psychiatrist would have learned had he proceeded further, had been one of the great loves of Lowry's life. A friend during the Cambridge days, Dr. Ralph Case, recalls:

> His sense of rhythm and phrasing was impeccable — he had that subtle something which every true jazz fan instantly recognizes. . . . Where jazz was concerned, his taste was, in my view, impeccable. . . . I would say that Bix was Malcolm's chief love among jazz musicians of the time . . . Closely linked with Bix, of course, was Frankie Trumbauer . . . 'Clarinet Marmalade', 'Singin' the Blues', 'Ostrich Walk', 'Way down Yonder in New Orleans', 'River Boat Shuffle', . . . all of these were like manna from heaven to Malcolm . . .

Lowry also favoured another all-white jazz group, The Memphis Five (active between 1923 and 1928) in their recordings of "Lovey Lee", "How Come You Do Me Like You Do?", "Beale Street Blues"; and later, a group of Toscanini's symphony musicians who called themselves The New Friends of Rhythm, and their recording of "Bach Bay Blues".

Dr. Case continues:

> . . . his [taste] was unerring in picking out the gold from the dross — he had no time for corny or pretentious numbers . . .

And Gerald Noxon, writing in the Lowry issue of *Prairie Schooner*, says:

> [Lowry] was passionately fond of jazz . . . I had a phonograph; a small but

respectable collection of jazz records...mostly blues, for which Malcolm and I shared a particular fondness.

According to prominent jazz critic Marshall Stearns, jazz is associated with protest and rebellion and identification with the underdog. Bix and his fellow white, Midwestern musicians ". . . sacrificed ease and relaxation for tension and drive. . . . They had read some of the literature of the twenties . . . and their revolt against their own middle-class background tended to be conscious." Across the Atlantic, the young Lowry, engaged in a similar turmoil, set to writing as Bix had turned to his music. *Ultramarine*, what later became *Lunar Caustic*, *Under the Volcano*, "Elephant and Colosseum", all feature the protagonist's identification with the dispossessed, the "philosophers", the "poor in spirit", the gentle animals, the *borrachos*, and the peons who bear the entire burden of civilization on their backs. Love of jazz was really another facet of Lowry's romanticism which extended later to his fondness for the simple lives of the Manx fishermen, their unsentimental faith, and their hymns. "But I was attached romantically to those days," says the musician-hero, recalling "Prohibition" and the "Jazz Age", in "The Forest Path to the Spring". For the older man jazz came to represent youth itself. So much for the psychological value of free association.

As a writer, Lowry often attempted to put prose to work as music. In fact, he compared his novel to "a kind of symphony . . . a kind of opera . . . hot music . . . a song", and referred continuously to "chords being resolved", "contrapuntal dialogue", and the like. One chapter, he says, "closes with a dying fall, like the end of some guitar piece of Ed Lang's. . . ." And, "the best kind of novel" — he confides to friend James Stern — is that which is "bald and winnowed, like Sibelius, and that makes an odd but splendid din, like Bix Beiderbecke." So that when he told his wife that "the early records had tremendous influence on his style of writing," he apparently knew what he was about. Only the slightest familiarity with music is necessary to see that his works are shot through with such purely musical techniques as reiterated refrain, aria, and the particular influence of Debussy on the alliterative, rhythmic, and onomonopeic effects used to describe nature, the sea, wilderness. From the earliest writing on there is a consistent identification between music, sound, and word. In *Ultramarine*, for example, ". . . down in the engine room three submarine

146

notes floated up and were followed by the jangling of the telegraph, while the engine changed key." Bells on a ship's bridge — "*tin-tin*: *tin-tin*" — recall the memory of goat bells, "tinkle tonkle tankle tunk", and pure young love, which is soon to be pitted against the lure of sin at a port whose name itself is musically related to the young hero's thoughts: "Tsang-Tsang". Memory, love, fear — all are associated with sounds, the creaking music of the ship's winches, the bells, the engines, a violin's notes blown in the wind from another ship docked nearby. And since Lowry's writing was all so closely autobiographical, the young sailor hero of *Ultramarine*, not surprisingly, plays the "taropatch".

Music has its daemonic aspects: the young boy's first encounter with a prostitute is accompanied by a jazz number ironically entitled "Dead Man Blues", for Dana Hilliot/Malcolm Lowry was then virtually obsessed with the fear of death by venereal disease.

Over and over again we find countless references to jazz — even tiny "inside" favours to jazz fans are interspersed throughout; tidbits like "Trumbaugh: named after Trumbauer — Frankie. Beiderbecke, et al." in "Through the Panama" or the nickname for his hero's wife in "Elephant and Colosseum": "Lovey (her nickname came from Lovey Lee, an old recording by the Memphis Five)" or in "The Forest Path to the Spring": "One evening on the way back from the spring for some reason I suddenly thought of a break by Bix in Frankie Trumbauer's record of "Singin' the Blues" that had always seemed to me to express a moment of the most pure spontaneous happiness...."[1]

And so it goes in story after story, novels, manuscripts for future stories and novels — innumerable allusions to jazz which finally culminate in a discernible pattern wherein the chaos and despair in the minds of Lowry's protagonists suddenly merge into order during a brief moment of illumination and joy. Like the pattern of Dixieland music itself, each story in *Hear Us O Lord From Heaven Thy Dwelling Place* begins slowly, almost mournfully, and builds in its sorrow until it seems almost too much to bear — then just as suddenly, it explodes in a climax of joy and hopefulness. This stylistic signature is best illustrated in its earliest and therefore its crudest form at the end of *Ultramarine*, Lowry's first novel:

> And all at once the maelstrom of noise, of tangled motion, of shining steel in his mind was succeeded by a clear perception of the meaning of the pitiless regularity of those moving bars; the jiggering levers began to keep time to a queer tune Hilliot had unconsciously fitted to their chanting, and he saw that at last the interdependence of rod grasping rod, of shooting straight line seizing curved

arms ... had become related to his own meaning and his own struggles. At last there dawned upon him a reason for his voyage ...

Here in the young boy's soliloquy of reconciliation to the sea is the embryo of the dying Consul's — albeit illusory — "vision" of the perfect pattern of existence at the close of *Under the Volcano*, also rendered largely in musical terms.

> Mozart was it? The Siciliana ... No, it was something funereal, of Gluck's perhaps, from *Alcestis*. Yet there was a Bach-like quality to it. Bach? A clavichord, heard from far away, in England in the seventeenth century. England. The chords of a guitar too, half lost, mingled with the distant clamour of a waterfall and what sounded like the cries of love.

Lowry peppered his works with references to Beiderbecke, Lang, Venuti and others, utilizing his expert knowledge of their musician's style to create metaphors, moods, even at times structuring his own stories within their formal influence. If the reader happened to be unfamiliar with analogies comparing a beautiful day to a Joe Venuti record (*Under the Volcano*) or a newsboy's cry to a piece of jazz mounting towards a break ("The Bravest Boat") so much the worse for that reader. This was part of Lowry's vocabulary (as were many other far more esoteric subjects like occultism, Indian legend, and the Blakean excesses of drink) so that ". . . to anyone who knew Malcolm intimately, it was inevitable that jazz should be tied with, indeed a part of his literary output" (Dr. Case).

Three of Lowry's literary hero-mouthpieces are in fact jazz musicians: the nameless narrator of "Forest Path", Bill Plantagenet of *Lunar Caustic*, and the Consul's half brother/alter ego, Hugh in *Under the Volcano*. Inevitably, some working knowledge of Lowry's jazz background is necessary in order to understand these characters, the conflicts presented and, in the case of *Under the Volcano*, the structure of the plot itself. "The Forest Path to the Spring" concerns a jazz musician who has given up the debilitating night life of the clubs for the wholesome life in nature — in other words, has exchanged death for life.

> Before I had married, and after I left the sea, I had been a jazz musician, but my health had been ruined by late hours and one-night stands all over the hemisphere. Now I had given up this life for the sake of our marriage and was making a new one — a hard thing for a jazz musician when he loves jazz as much as I.

With the help of his old colleagues, the narrator obtains a piano and is thus able to earn a small living by composing and titling jazz tunes. Things go well for a time; the narrator learns how to cope with the rough ways of the wilderness — specifically, the fetching of water for the cottage from the source of a spring, which requires a rather long walk through the forest. Like other Lowry heroes, the narrator falls gradually into a state of despair, undergoes a dark night of the soul (embodied in the absolute loathing he conceives for his water-carrying task) and is very suddenly bolted by a recollection of a Bix Beiderbecke solo into a "moment of the most pure spontaneous happiness" and the desire "to do something good". Goodness is synonymous with creation and the very Protestant emphasis on work, as evil is associated with torpor and neglect; so that our jazzman determines now to write "a symphony in which I would incorporate among other things . . . the true feeling and rhythm of jazz. . . . The theme was suggested probably by my thoughts of *cleansing* and *purgation* and *renewal*" (Italics mine). Here the power of music assumes religious overtones, when the very core of suffering (in this case the initial abandonment of the so-called "jazz life", and its resumption under entirely new circumstances) becomes a force for regeneration. Lowry was constantly placing his characters in hell so that they might reach heaven: compare Bix himself and countless other jazz musicians who were both exalted and destroyed by their work.

The hero of *Lunar Caustic* is not only a jazz musician but an alcoholic as well. As if things weren't bad enough, Bill Plantagenet is unemployed, an alien adrift in New York, and hallucinating. The breakup of his band in England is consonant symbolically with the breakup of his marriage and of his total personality. The inability to play, that is to work as a musician, is tantamount to disintegration.

"Bill Plantagenet and his Seven Hot Cantabs . . ." he introduces himself to the psychiatrist at Bellevue, where he has voluntarily committed himself, "We went a treat in Cambridge . . . we were all right with our first records, too, we took that seriously. . . . You know you people get sentimental over England from time to time. . . . Well, this was the other way round. Only it was Eddie Lang and Joe Venuti and the death of Bix . . ." that presumably brought this Englishman to America in the hope of patching up the pieces of his own life. But even here in the madhouse he is rejected by the only people who can understand his music: a Negro patient named Battle is infuriated when Bill sits down to play the piano. "Something in the rhythm of his [Battle's] blood, it seemed, did not like Bill's music; not because it was alien music, it was precisely because it sounded too cognate that he would not conform to it." Bill's one attempt to communicate results in what was known in jazz parlance as a *cutting contest*, where two musicians "battle it out" for first place. Bill plays "In a Mist" and "Singin' the Blues". "He played Frankie Trumbauer's old version fast." The tension builds as the appropriately named Battle sets up a counter song about the sinking of the *Titanic*, and a discussion about black versus white whales ensues among the patients.

"Glancing at Battle for approval", Bill launches into "Clarinet Marmalade" — only to be eyed "stonily" by the Negro. " 'Say listen,' Battle demanded, 'let's have some truckin' — don't you know any truckin' . . .' " (i.e. backing up a soloist on the piano.) Suddenly Bill is pushed from the piano by a "mental defective" who somehow manages to bring all the patients, even the truculent Battle, together in a symphony of discord. Symbolically defeated, the lonely alcoholic Englishman is soon after dismissed from the hospital as an alien. His moment of self recognition comes when, once again down and out on the street, it suddenly becomes clear that two pathetic creatures left behind, a senile old man and an angel-faced schizophrenic boy, are his only friends in the world. His music rejected even by the insane, Plantagenet stumbles out drunk and ironically "free", into the streets of the city.

In contrast to "The Forest Path to the Spring", jazz in this novella is used to depict the lonely disintegration of an unsuccessful artist and — by extension — the isolation of all men. *Lunar Caustic* is perhaps the closest Lowry came to presenting a written tribute to the tragedy of Bix Beiderbecke's life and his own.

I T IS GENERALLY AGREED that Hugh and the Consul are fictionalized versions of the young and older Malcolm Lowry. In fact Hugh's musical shenanigans, the Bolowski music publishing fiasco, and the songwriting, are thinly veiled autobiography stemming from a period during his Cambridge career when, according to Dr. Case, Lowry and a friend named Ronnie Hill "wrote a number called 'I've Said Good-bye to Shanghai' which was actually printed but was never sold. . . . I think, though I am not sure, that Malcolm and Ronnie did pay for the printing or 'publishing'."

Biographically interesting details such as these can only furnish half the story behind so brilliant a novel as *Under the Volcano*. Still more fascinating, however, is the way in which such a complex novel was put together. Each time I read it I found some new skein to trace. In my book on Lowry and the Cabbala I pointed out that the construction of *Volcano* with its twelve chapters is based to some extent on the Zohar with its emphasis on the mystical number twelve. Here I would like to note that the blues form in jazz is also based on a twelve-bar construction. Being a connoisseur of blues and an amateur song writer himself, Lowry could really have meant it when he referred to his book as a jazz tune. Introduced in the slow blues manner, the first chapter of the novel is devoted to a lament for the dead — the Mexican souls abroad on the Day of the Dead, and more specifically, a lament for the dead Consul. To remind us in the old manner of the Negro mourners in New Orleans, Lowry has Laruelle hear "a despondent American tune, the 'St. Louis Blues,' or some such . . ." This first chapter states the "blues" or tragic theme of the novel as the Dixieland musicians playing a mournful tune on their way to a funeral state the theme of death. Dr. Vigil and Laruelle provide the chorus (they are choral in the classical Greek sense, too) and the rest of the novel unfolds as a series of variations and explanations of their commentary.

Geoffrey's, Yvonne's, and Hugh's individual "stories", their points of view, might be compared with the improvisations of soloists, but the theme is resolved, in the final chapter, on the same note that ends the first chapter: *dolente, dolore* — the ringing of the bell for the souls of the dead.

Under the Volcano is in many ways a catalogue of human suffering, much as the blues are. The harmony in the novel is provided, however, not by the crude stringing of guitars (although fictional guitar stringing occurs consistently throughout) but by stream of consciousness techniques and by the imposed contingencies of the outer world on the mind: Peter Lorre cinema posters, overheard snatches of conversation in a bar, recurring advertisements for sporting events, etc. The final chapter of the novel is the closest possible literary version of a complicated harmonic piece of jazz music (Malcolm used to play one of his songs on the piano in "the advanced and improbable key of six flats!", says Dr. Case) that drives to a terrifically charged "hot" finish. Lowry also had the musician's knack for establishing a theme — for example, the bull throwing at Tomalin — very early through Geoffrey's eyes, say, and then picking it up again from Yvonne's point of view. This is similar also to the jazz soloist's variation on a melody; with the Consul playing lead trumpet throughout, Hugh, Yvonne and Laruelle function as "sidemen" who act and react to his signals.

The older jazz form concentrates on the statement of the chorus, solo improvisation, and often a kind of counterpoint that occurs between two instruments, the clarinet and trumpet perhaps; these instruments will "talk" to each other or sometimes against each other after the solos, building up toward the final chorus when all the musicians play ensemble. This is neatly accomplished by Lowry in chapters ten, eleven, and twelve, which culminate in the frenetic climax of the novel. In chapter ten the competing "instruments" are Hugh and Geoffrey locked in an argument ostensibly about Communism. Hugh is trying to explain why he believes in it while Geoffrey tries to describe his own drunkard's plight.

> " 'See here, Geoffrey —'
> " 'See here, old bean . . . to have against you Franco, or Hitler is one thing, but to have Actinium, Argon, Beryllium, Dysprosium" etc., etc.
> " 'Look here, Geoff —'
> " 'Ruthenium, Samarium, Silicon,' " etc., etc.
> " 'See here —' " etc., etc.

The musical nature of this "cutting contest" strikes one immediately with Hugh's "Look here" and See here" punctuating in short blasts Geoffrey's long, rhythmic enumeration of the elements. The Consul is "playing" hot and fast; even Cervantes, the cafe owner, joins in with the traditional pattern of *call and response* that underlies all jazz forms.

> " 'Cervantes . . . you are Oaxaqueñan?'
> " 'No, señor . . . I am Tlaxcalan, Tlaxcala.'
> " 'You are . . . Well, hombre, and are there not stricken in years trees in Tlaxcala?'
> " 'Sí, sí, hombre. Stricken in years trees. Many trees.' "

Suddenly a man with a guitar appears and begins to play. Geoffrey, who has not finished his "solo", says: " 'Tell him to go away. . . .' " And then, as if to confirm the underlying musical foundation of the scene, the Consul actually "sees" his performance in terms of:

> . . . a piece on the piano, it was like that little bit in seven flats on the black keys . . . like that little piece one had learned, so laboriously, years ago, only to forget whenever one particularly wanted to play it, until one day one got drunk in such a way that one's fingers themselves recalled the combination and, miraculously, perfectly, unlocked the wealth of melody . . .

The theme of the final chapter opens on discord: a mixture of "*I'm just a country b-boy*", drunken references to Mozart, the imagined plaintive cries of Yvonne through her letters, a fiddler playing "The Star Spangled Banner", "It's a Long Way to Tipperary", builds to a simulated resolution in order when the Consul "hears" Bach as his life ebbs away, and finally ends in a very literal dying fall (cf. Ed Lang's guitar) as Geoffrey is flung down into the ravine.

Corroborating these musical intentions in his *Letters*, Lowry sums up by saying: "Is it too much to say that all these chords, struck and resolved, while no reader can possibly apprehend them on first or even fourth reading consciously, nevertheless vastly contribute *unconsciously* to the final weight of the book?"

Since jazz is not at all intended to be "weighty", yet is nonetheless both gay and tragic at once, and since the same can be said of Malcolm Lowry, I will close with a humorous musical anecdote. It was a warm summer night in Dollarton. Malcolm and Margerie Lowry were seated on the platform of their shack that led to the water; they were feeling fine after a few drinks, and were enjoying the lovely night. Malcolm began to play hot jazz on his taropatch, then he started dancing to his own music, which grew hotter and hotter, until he "finally danced right bang off the end of the pier and into the water, uke and all."[3]

(1970)

FOOTNOTES

[1] "In fact this solo is usually considered one of the three most celebrated solos in jazz history.... It is a solo of intense, brooding beauty, carefully built up to a typical tumbling break in the middle with a surprise explosion after it. There was hardly a contemporary white musician of jazz pretensions who didn't learn it by heart." George Avakian, Liner Notes on *Bix Beiderbecke Story*, Vol. II, Columbia Records.

[2] "He said many many years ago ... that Bach was the background for all classical jazz." (Margerie Lowry)

[3] I am indebted for this anecdote to my friend Margerie Lowry, to whom I express my general gratitude for her help in gathering information for this article; I express my gratitude also to Dr. Ralph Case of London for his full and generously transmitted recollections of Malcolm Lowry's "jazz days".

RECOLLECTIONS OF
MALCOLM LOWRY

William McConnell

O<small>N MAY</small> 14th, 1927, Malcolm Lowry was 17 years old. On that day the Liverpool correspondent for the *London Evening News* interviewed him just before he sailed on the cargo steamer *Pyrrhus* as a deckhand at 50/- per month. He told the correspondent: "No silk-cushion youth for me. I want to see the world and rub shoulders with its oddities, and get some experience of life before I go back to Cambridge University." The Correspondent interviewed his rich cotton broker father and his mother, too, but only her comments are on record: "He is bent on a literary career, and his short story writing is all to him," said Mrs. Lowry, when the ship had left.

On his return from Port Said, Shanghai and Yokohama Lowry was again interviewed, this time by *The Daily Mail*. With characteristic candour he announced he didn't intend to go to sea again, since a fourteen hour day, chipping paint, scrubbing decks and polishing brass was not to his liking. He said he intended to go on to university, compose fox-trots and write fiction.

One of his intentions was realized, as we know, for Malcolm Lowry wrote, among many other works, one of the great novels of the twentieth century, *Under the Volcano*. Despite the early experience of his four months' voyage as deckhand, he returned to sea, travelling to every ocean, beachcombed in the South Seas, settled for troubled spates in Mexico, Haiti, Germany until he finally found, again close to the sea, a waterfront shack at Dollarton, ten miles from Vancouver, where he could write and live in his own peculiar, uneasy peace.

It was during this last period of his life that I met Malcolm and his wife, Margerie, (who published many fictional works under her maiden name, Margerie Bonner). It was at a cocktail party at the Caulfield home of Alan Crawley. A. J. M. Smith and the American poet, Theodore Roethke, had persuaded Malcolm to attend. He was pathologically shy and any group of more than four

154

usually caused perspiration to drip from his face, but on this occasion there was no shyness. It was a gathering of writers, of like beings, of natural and mutual acceptance. He hated literary people; to the same degree he accepted and loved those he felt were dedicated to literature. Quite often this blind acceptance caused him self-hurt and disappointment, but more often it created deep friendship.

Physically, Lowry was a powerful man: short, broad-shouldered, with a tremendous chest. His gait was rolling, whether as accommodation to his bulk or the result of years at sea, or simply the acquisition of an imagined habit, I don't know. He was fair-headed, with muscular arms and small feet. Most impressive of all were his intense blue eyes which looked into and through your own, which gazed into the distance, which altered in hue as his mood varied.

Most of his life from the time he left university until he discovered Dollarton was spent in physical activity in odd corners of the globe, but, like the scattered notes which he wrote on bus transfers, cigarette papers or any other chance piece of paper, all of his life was lived for metamorphosis into short story, poem or novel. He could discard nothing and, consequently, writing to him was not the usual casting for idea, figure of speech, or character portrayal, but rather a painful, tortuous process of selection and arrangement.

He had that rare (and rather frightening) gift of near total recall. I saw him sometimes after intervals of several months. For the first five minutes he would stare contemplatively across Burrard Inlet at the evening outline of Burnaby Mountain, then reflectively at a gull sweeping low over the water, then finally at me. Out of the air with magic, it seemed to one like myself who had little memory whatever, he would recount word-perfect an argument we had had on our previous meeting. He would review exactly what each of us had said, then quietly announce that he had been (or I had been, it doesn't matter) in error in a particular statement. Accuracy, even on trivial matters, was an obsession.

This accuracy was one of the strengthening qualities of his writing. By exact physical depiction, razor-edged characterization, evocation of mood, he had some alchemy which would make each line true in detail, yet with layers of meaning which could be peeled off by the reader without the onion becoming smaller. In his great novel, *Under the Volcano*, this is revealed in many pages. For example, I recall Malcolm describing to me how, when a young man in Wales, he had come across an amusing insertion in a Visitors' Book in a hotel. He described it on several occasions, each time not really adding anything, yet casting a different spell over the event on each telling. Consider my delight, then, when I encountered it in another guise in the novel:

"Climbed the Parson's Nose," one had written, in the visitors' book at the little Welsh rock-climbing hotel, "in twenty minutes. Found the rocks very easy." "Came down the Parson's Nose," some immortal wag had added a day later, "in twenty seconds. Found the rocks very hard." .... So now, as I approach the second half of my life, unheralded, unsung, and without a guitar, I am going back to sea again: perhaps these days of waiting are more like that droll descent, to be survived in order to repeat the climb. At the top of the Parson's Nose you could walk home to tea over the hills if you wished, just as the actor in the Passion Play can get off his cross and go home to his hotel for a Pilsener.

We walked along the beach one late afternoon — a warm afternoon when the tide was full, the salt-chuck quiet as if it had been fed to satiety and didn't want the never-changing chore of accommodating itself to the tug of the moon. We were having one of those intense and enjoyable silences which can cement each to the other without any mortar of words. We came across the oil-encrusted corpse of a seagull. I knew, of course, how passionately fond of birds Malcolm was (a well-marked pocket-size volume of Peterson's *Field Guide* was usually beside him) and I made some remark about someone's criminality in dumping bunker oil in the harbour. Malcolm nodded, then pointed without a word to the flares of the oil refineries on the other shore, his hand sweeping even further to indicate the smog which sawmills in Vancouver's False Creek were emitting to soot the land-scape. Later, when we had doubled back up the hillside and through the ever-green forest, his fingers felt the new sharp green needles of the young hemlocks and he contemplatively dug with his toe at the dropped needles which had con-tributed to the forest loam. A deep observer, he believed nothing was or could be wasted in nature and that death itself was necessary for creation.

Was this knowledge, perhaps, the reason for Lowry's bouts of alcoholism? Unlike most of his friends I never saw him during such times. He did discuss everything but the reason for them with me candidly and simply (there was no false pride, no pantomiming of excuse, but simple direct statement). On several occasions I know his fear of groups triggered him off. Once he arrived at an august tea party staggering and all but speechless, wanting to hammer ragtime on the piano instead of being listened to with respect and awe. There were other occasions when he was alone and his loneliness simply could not be borne. I sus-pect that sometimes the creativity which constantly welled up from within himself could not be channelled as he wished it and had to be deadened by some ano-dyne. He didn't possess the routine and familiar antidotes with which the majority of us are equipped. During these frightening periods his understanding and devoted wife and the few friends, such as Einar and Muriel Neilson of Bowen Island, to whom he turned like a child, carried him through and, more important, beyond, during the even more bitter period of contriteness.

He told me one day that during the long months when he had written *Under the Volcano* he had not taken a drink even of wine, though he had been staying with a friend who had vineyards and made wine while he wrote. I mentioned earlier how every tag end of event was of importance to him, and somehow incorporated into his writing. This was true even of his attempts at forgetfulness, his wild occasional descents to escape the unbidden imagery he could not momentarily harness. He describes just such a period experienced by the Consul:

...... Why then should he be sitting in the bathroom? Was he asleep? dead? passed out? Was he in the bathroom now or half an hour ago? Was it night? Where were the others? But now he heard some of the others' voices on the porch. Some of the others? It was just Hugh and Yvonne, of course, for the doctor had gone. Yet for a moment he could have sworn the house had been full of people; why it was still this morning, or barely afternoon, only 12:15 in fact by his watch. At eleven he'd been talking to Mr. Quincey. "Oh .... Oh." The Consul groaned aloud .... It came to him he was supposed to be getting ready to go to Tomalin. But how had he managed to persuade anyone he was sober enough to go to Tomalin? And why, anyhow, Tomalin?

A procession of thoughts like little elderly animals filed through the Consul's mind, and in his mind too he was steadily crossing the porch again, as he had done an hour ago, immediately after he'd seen the insect flying away out of the cat's mouth.

Unlike most of us, Malcolm had not lost the wise-eyed innocence of childhood. In fact, many of the incidents of his childhood remained in his mind vivid as current events. He told me on several occasions, for example, of a nurse his wealthy family employed when he was very young. She had loved his older brother and to his horror hated him. Once she had wheeled his cart along the cliff-edge, high above the rolling sea. He described with quiet exactitude her features as she leaned over with a blanket to smother him, how he screamed (the exact key), and then the saving running footsteps of his favoured older brother which interrupted the scene.

I used to steal glances at my seven year old son when Malcolm and Margerie visited the cottage by the lake in which we were then living. His features were as mobile as Malcolm's when Malcolm was talking, as intent, and as unspoiled by conditioned attitudes. Those two instinctively understood what each other was feeling as well as taking in the surface articulation.

Don't let me suggest that Malcolm was sombre. He had a huge Rabelaisian sense of humour and, rare quality, could laugh with gusto at himself. One afternoon we were visiting Malcolm and Margerie at their shack. It was several months after he had injured his leg badly when he fell from his wharf on to lowtide rocks (preoccupied with dialogue, so he said, dialogue to finish off a discussion he, Margerie, my wife and myself had had months before). He described the horror of the Catholic hospital where he had been taken (the cowled nuns, for some reason, were the opposite to Sisters of Charity to his pain-wracked mind) and the even greater horror of later visiting his orthopædic specialist who sat examining his leg and remarking he might lose it. Malcolm graphically detailed the whole room, his utterances of despair that he might lose the leg, then the asceptic smile of the doctor who casually remarked, as he reached behind and brought out a new nickel shining artificial limb and stroked it, that it was as good as a natural one for the classical case of amputation on another patient he had. Desultory talk followed this devilish recount, then Malcolm, who was always fascinated by the law, asked me whether I had had any interesting law cases recently. I was young in my profession then and, perhaps over enthusiastically, I described a Motor Manslaughter case I had defended. I described the difficulties. The accused was on the wrong side of a straight road, he had spent the afternoon drinking beer in a pub, and the police had found a half-finished bottle of whisky in his truck after the accident. In recounting all the evidence against my client, then finally the jury's acquittal verdict, I gleefully remarked, "It was a classical case!" I looked up and there was Malcolm stroking an imaginary artificial steel limb, murmuring "classical case", then he erupted into roars of gargantuan laughter. His thesis of "never trust an expert" probably had some merit.

Malcolm personally knew a number of great writers who admired his work and communicated their admiration to him. One of his special friends was Conrad Aiken. Aiken recognised his genius long before the public success of *Under the Volcano*. While still at Cambridge some of Lowry's short stories were published in America, and in 1932 his first novel *Ultramarine* received a rather indifferent public response. It was during this period that Aiken encouraged and stimulated him.

He had known well, while in England, Dylan Thomas. Upon the occasion when Thomas first came to Vancouver for a public poetry reading, Malcolm, the shyest man I have ever known, remarked laconically that Dylan Thomas for all his flamboyant public personality, was really a very shy person. After Dylan

Thomas's reading a reception was arranged to which the Lowrys and ourselves were invited. Despite Malcolm's dislike of people in groups ("individuals lose their most precious possession — their identity"), and his antipathy towards 'literary people' ("they don't write, they talk aseptically about it as if there were no bloody birth pangs and the work emerges well-scrubbed") he wanted to meet Dylan. In the many-roomed converted old house where the reception was held both were for a long time in separate rooms, both being lionized and hating it. At length friends managed to bring them together. They warmly clasped hands and Malcolm said simply: "Hullo, Dylan," while Dylan Thomas replied with equal shyness, "Hullo, Malcolm." In retrospect I feel similar inner fires were burning in each because they could not render the whole of their experience into a creative mould.

In Malcolm's relaxed periods he strummed a huge repertoire of songs, chanties and tunes he had composed (including a lively national anthem) on a battered ukelele, and he was never so happy as when he was immersed in this music of his own making, whether bawdy Spanish tunes picked up in some waterfront bistro in North Africa, or plaintive Chinese rise and fall he had heard in Singapore. Hours would pass delightfully, for he took it for granted you shared his happiness.

After the publication of *Under the Volcano*, Malcolm and his wife travelled for a year, visiting Haiti, England and the Continent. With his habitual generosity he shared his royalties with the many he encountered who claimed to be able to put words on to paper. When he returned to his beloved shack at Dollarton there were periods of acute financial want and it was during one of these periods there occurred a minor event which highlighted two of his characteristics — naiveté and the ability to laugh at himself.

About this time one of our popular national magazines printed, as an advertisement for a bank, a single-page short story headed: "We Printed This Because We Liked It." At its conclusion there was an invitation to other writers to make submissions.

Many months later Malcolm laughingly told me of his submission. It started off as a well-planned anecdote but somehow it became longer and longer. Feverish weeks were spent as the anecdote dilated and expanded into the eventually completed whole — a piece of work which would have required ten issues of the whole magazine instead of a single page. He had waited patiently for weeks to receive the bank's cheque before he gradually realized the violent sea-change his creativity had caused. Fortunately, about this time royalties from some of the translated editions of *Under the Volcano* began trickling in.

Many are generous, as he was, with material possessions, but few extend the intellectual generosity he was capable of. It mattered not to Malcolm whether someone was famous or unknown, skilled in the craft of writing or a fumbling tyro. He, who knew how difficult it was to piece together common words so they sang and wreathed in rich meaning, gave consideration, time, advice (but never didactically, always subjectively) and encouragement to all who asked for it. He not only loved language and the individual warp and woof rendered by a writer, but revered it. He, a master, considered himself a tyro and anyone who tackled the same task with love he viewed as a potential genius.

Malcolm's relationship with his wife was far more than the customary one. They were partners in everything they did, sharing the successes or the periods of actual want with equal zest. He was proud of her attractive gaiety and her theatrical (she had been an actress) manner. More important, he was as concerned with her writing as he was with his own — and as proud of it. Margerie's opinion was constantly sought and considered. Equally, her concern and consideration for his welfare, her honest and penetrating appraisals of his work, supplied Malcolm with a reserve of strength and stimulation which always carried him through the bleak non-productive periods every writer encounters. Margerie possessed that rare quality — intellectual honesty and forthrightness. They admired and respected as well as loved each other.

I recall Malcolm's delight when I introduced him to T. E. Lawrence's *Seven Pillars of Wisdom*. I was a bit taken aback at his enthusiasm until I realised that Lawrence's writing resembled his own in its rare concern with metaphysics. "I must write to him," he told me. I reminded him that Lawrence had been dead for decades. Malcolm ignored this, for to him a writer never died. He accepted it on the surface, of course, so he improvised long verbal letters instead which enlivened our walks. The symbolism in Lowry's work is not confined to the work itself. It was part of his daily life. His world was peopled with black and white forces. His daily swim (even when light skim ice scummed the surface of the deep North Arm) was not merely a swim but a metaphysical experience. I've mentioned the gas flares at the cracking plant. For hours he would discuss them, not as hot crackling oil flames spurting into the evening's darkness, but as living sentient forces which peopled his world. In the same way the Consul, towards the end of *Under the Volcano*, symbolically invests in a calendar.

He saw again in his mind's eye that extraordinary picture on Laruelle's wall, Los Borrachones, only now it took on a somewhat different aspect. Mightn't it have another meaning, that picture, unintentional as its humour, beyond the symbolically obvious? He saw those people like spirits appearing to grow more free, more separate, their distinctive noble faces more distinctive, more noble the higher they ascended into the light; those florid people resembling huddled fiends, becoming more like each other, more joined together, more as one fiend, the further down they hurtled into the darkness.

His last novel (unfortunately the middle section was taken out and never replaced) was typical of this.[1] For several years there had been recurrent rumours that the waterfront shacks, including his own, were to be bulldozed and the occupant squatters forced out of the beach strip. This had a terrible effect upon him. Here, as I said, he had found his uneasy peace. For a month he and Margerie had searched the Gulf Islands and Vancouver Island for an alternate home. The novel was, on the surface, about the search for a home and dispossession, but the recurrent symbolism of many facets raced through it contrapuntally. Just as *Under the Volcano* had been written and rewritten four times (once completely rewritten in a month when the previous draft had perished in a fire), so did this final and tremendous work undergo many changes and alterations.

One afternoon — early, about 2:30 — he started to read the first draft of his last novel to myself, Margerie and my wife. The typescript was interlineated with his spidery written additions and changes. He would finish a page and, without dropping a word, walk into the bedroom to pick up a scrap of waste paper on which was an inserted paragraph. We had brought a bottle of gin. As it was a festive and important occasion he had bought two himself. Margerie, my wife and I had several drinks, but were spellbound after that by his resonant voice and the wonder of his prose. He read on and on, drinking in sips of straight gin, without slurring a syllable or slighting a word. Finally, at 2:30 in the morning, he finished the last paragraph, the three bottles empty. My wife and I were terribly exhausted, but elated. When we got up to leave Malcolm was immersed in a paragraph he wanted to rewrite again, but rose to light our way up the trail with warmness and thanks, as if it had been we who had performed the favour. "God bless you," he would always say, instead of "Goodbye". This is the Malcolm we'll remember, and the one to be seen in his verse and prose.

Last month we drove by on the cliff road overlooking the former Dollarton shacks. Bulldozers were matting the underbrush to make way for a park. The

[1] *October Ferry to Gabriola*, published (1970), since this article was written. ED.

squatters' shacks, Malcolm's included, had long since disappeared. We were sad and spoke retrospectively, then brightened, remembering the seagull dead from oil, the dropped needles which made the forest floor. He surpassed all of these, Malcolm did, for during his lifetime, not after it, he created life from his own.

(1960)

LIFE WITH
MALCOLM LOWRY

Maurice J. Carey

(Edited by Anthony R. Kilgallin)

(Readers of Malcolm Lowry's Selected Letters will remember that his early letters from Vancouver in 1939 and 1940 bore the address of Sergeant Major Maurice Carey. Now, 30 years later, Maurice Carey had written his recollections of their relationship, and the following pages are an extract from his notes. They vividly confirm the impression of Lowry's constricted and dependent situation owing to financial stringencies and to the conditions imposed by his family on aiding him at the time. It is well to note that — if one can judge from his letters — Lowry's view of the situation was somewhat different from Carey's. ED.)

My MEETING with Malcolm Lowry was not in the least auspicious. It was summertime in 1939. I and a lawyer friend, involved in the defence of an impaired driver, were seated in a local cocktail lounge discussing the pros and cons of over-indulgence in alcohol. We had warmed up to the subject of gin, and its detrimental effects, particularly on the brain, when a man at an adjacent table detached himself from his obviously drunken companion and, with a glass of colourless liquid held aloft, proclaimed that in no circumstances should gin be drunk except in its raw and naked form — "with — forgive me if I resort to the plebeian — a few beers for chasers."

This unkempt individual propelled himself to our table with a minimum of economy. After apologizing for the intrusion, he introduced himself and, with a slight backward fling of his hand and a flick of the wrist, he marked finis to his drink. Malcolm Lowry then subsided into the chair he had pre-empted at our table and, without rising, shook hands with us. He had the grip of a pipe wrench.

This seaman-cum-landlubber was of squat stature, with a belly gone to pot, the chest capacity of a mastodon, and the arms of a pigmy. He wore a well-worn navy sweat shirt, grubby cotton slacks and sandals. His spasmodic pulling and plucking at his clothing suggested that he had trouble keeping himself intact or that he had miniature company — which he had not.

In a moderate, highly confidential and refined English voice he settled down to relate his experiences at sea, where he informed us he had shipped out as deckhand or passenger on everything from a bathtub to a 20,000 ton tramp.

For several hours I had the opportunity to study this man with a camel's capacity. His disordered thatch of dusty, red-tinged hair required the services of a barber — and he would have to be an expert barber. There was lots of space between his ears. His close-set eyes squinted through half-closed lids; one eyelid drooped lower than the other; the eye he disclosed was perhaps a little calculating, but mostly humorous. The week-old gingerbread beard seemed to have sprouted reluctantly and in patches, as does a newly-sown lawn. The unkempt sprigs of hair that made up his moustache did nothing for him but to accentuate the irregular teeth which arched to a point in front of a rather loosely hung mouth. That part of his high-cheeked, full-blown face I could see was beet-red; his sensitive nose belonged to a private investigator. It is odd, but positively true, that Malcolm's right hand was always half-open as though in readiness to grasp any sort of container that held spirits of wine. Actually, as I discovered afterwards, he had a condition known to medicos as a superficial fibroma; stranger still is the fact that I too suffer from the same deformity — in both hands!

Even before we ordered his first drink, Lowry apologized for having to miss his turn at treating, but solemnly declared that, somewhere about his person, he had a few cents which, if we didn't mind, he would keep in reserve for transportation and a morsel of food. We didn't mind at all. He was most concerned about people who "over-indulged" and "lost track of themselves". In the light of future happenings these were, indeed, prophetic remarks.

As the evening turned to nightfall, we decided to head for home. When we stood outside the hotel, Malcolm told me that although he had "a place in the country", he did not then feel capable of journeying so far, but that he had no alternative place to sleep. I took him home and put him in one of the spare rooms upstairs.

Early next morning he asked if he might have a drink. I was about to respond with hard liquor when I was astounded to hear him request: "Just a sip of aqua pura, if you don't mind!" And that, he said, was a firmly established habit of his.

"No matter how far-tilted out of equilibrium I become, I have nothing to do with Sir John Barleycorn in the morning." Then, with a slight pause, "unless of course I am still *non compos mentis* from the night before." And as he was, at that very moment, in that exact condition, he knocked back a nauseating slug of raw whisky.

During a serious chat that same morning, I asked him if he had hope of employment, to which he replied that he had "a bit of a job" to do. This "bit of a job" proved to be his magnum opus, *Under the Volcano* (which at that moment was "probably trampled underfoot somewhere in my cottage at Dollarton"), and with his hands raised, and a look of utter dejection clouding his face, he remarked: "Upon which I must shortly re-engage myself — or else!"

Several times I sloshed with him through oozing mud and wet tangled bush to the "cottage", which was situated on the rocky, log-strewn beach at Dollarton, on the North Shore beside Burrard Inlet. On the occasion of my first visit, my host, after huffing and puffing at a precariously shored-up stove, offered me a brew which he called Java, in a cup deeply embossed with a ring of left-over coffee. The decoction had the aroma of smoked cod, the consistency of dark brown calcamine, and the flavour of dissolved hell. After a great deal of searching we collected the finished chapters of his manuscript. The several visits I made to Dollarton convinced me, beyond doubt, that some of the material contained in his novel was siphoned out of the atmosphere of that grim and sordid bothy.

IT TOOK SEVERAL DAYS to pry from Malcolm the details of his current position, and how he had managed to survive so far into the year, following a dastardly winter. He admitted that he had been forced to dispose of a few of his personal effects (almost down to his greying underwear); it also transpired that at irregular times he had received money from his father in England. Being a benefactor of any derelict who was thirsty, he gave almost all of it away. "I was always damned glad to get rid of it," he remarked, "on account of the porous nature of my pockets."

Immediately prior to my meeting him, the flow of Malcolm's overseas remittances had dwindled from a mere dribble to practically nothing. A gentleman, whose name strangely was the same as mine and who was associated with various philanthropic endeavours, had enjoyed a lengthy friendship with Malcolm's father and had therefore undertaken to apportion to Malcolm the money he received at various times from Mr. Lowry. It was unfortunate that at the time of my meeting Malcolm, a feeling of bitter resentment and embarrassment which he had stirred in his father—whom he regarded with a deep and almost fanatical affection—combined with the disappointment aroused in Mr. Carey (who had made ardent but ineffectual attempts to rehabilitate Malcolm and steer him down a straight and narrow corridor) to make it extremely difficult for anyone to intercede in the matter. Mr. Lowry had almost reached the disowning stage, and Mr. Carey was fed up to the point of extreme indigestion!

After extracting from Lowry his firm and "irrevocable" promise of complete co-operation in all matters for the future, I telephoned Mr. Carey. Carefully avoiding the circumstances of our meeting, I managed to persuade that astute business executive to give us a hearing. Mr. Carey said at the time that he had tried often to detect even some slight sense of responsibility and congruity in Malcolm, but always in vain. Yet, though he felt it useless, he bade us: "Come along, any way."

The transformation of my friend, in preparation for the portentous confrontation, was a sight to behold! His unruly mop was shorn to civilized length; his face shaved to the smoothness of polished granite. The toothbrush moustache resisted the dull razor, and remained. Lowry donned my tweed sports coat over a sparkling white shirt — the sleeves tucked up because of his abbreviated arms. The ensemble was completed by a garish tie and a pair of trousers which a kind neighbour of the same size had donated. Lowry's fallen arches were encased in a pair of badly scuffed *huaraches* — about all he had left to remind him of his protracted stay in Mexico. He looked like a man who had reached the lowest level of human existence — had seen the dregs in the barrel — but with exemplary will-power had sneered at them and turned away.

When we arrived at his office, Mr. Carey appeared to be pleased to see Malcolm in such good shape; he examined him at great length as to his intentions, especially relating to his writing. Malcolm underwent the interrogation impassively. After I told Mr. Carey that I had been a Company Sergeant Major in World War I, he concluded that I was sufficient of a disciplinarian to undertake the task of trying to put Malcolm together again; an arrangement for him to stay with me and for payment of his sustenance occupied a few minutes.

Returned home, our guest settled down in the domestic scene, and right away showed a vast enthusiasm about the manuscript, a zeal of which up to then I had not suspected the existence. He collated the pages and within fifteen minutes, after having been warmly greeted by my wife and three children (upon whom he doted) he was deep in concentration. His slight hand deformity restricted him to just a couple of pages each day, yet, even though produced in slow motion, his output within a week was quite substantial.

On the occasion of my little daughter Carol's birthday, Malcolm, after a visit to a suburban store, proudly presented her with a taffy-striped kitten, which he brought forth from underneath his jacket. The pet had no more than lapped up the milk Malcolm had brought along, than a lady from a few houses down the street appeared to establish her legal claim to it. Glaring at Malcolm, she expressed in a few, exceedingly well-chosen words, her displeasure with people who kidnapped innocent cats. Malcolm's reply was muffled by chagrin. "Well, people should not allow their small cats to stray wild. I, madam, am a cat lover!" I have always had the feeling that the extent of the kitten's straying was from its home verandah to the front lawn.

After a few days Lowry elected to refer to me as his brother, which term he still applied to me when we met again several years later. He continued to be ever more enthusiastic about his writing, and spent many laborious hours at work, without a spot of drink. The goose hung high!

It was quite obvious from the start that the most pressing need as far as Malcolm was concerned was a typewriter, an instrument he later referred to as his "click-clacking conspirator." Taking a section of the hand-written manuscript with me, I called on Mr. Carey. In short order I obtained a requisition for an expensive Underwood machine. A quantity of typing paper and other necessary sundries were also purchased.

I began to feel that I was making headway in rehabilitating Malcolm. The whole household felt exuberant; but was it perhaps a trifle too soon? In any event I had, for a delightful change, a sober man on my hands. Malcolm, without liquor, now drank copious draughts of milk and soda pop, and chewed gum with the ferocity of a losing football coach. With regular meals and undisturbed rest, he became an entirely different man. He seemed to be possessed by a solitary, single purpose: to get off more chapters to the publishers, who were requesting them. His mind sparkled; he worked with inspired vigour, and rewrote long passages which had been written out of the grogginess of his earlier mental state.

One day, having to keep an appointment in the city, I left Malcolm diligently performing on the newly acquired "click-clacker". The first thing I noticed when I returned home was that the typewriter was missing and Malcolm nowhere in sight. Three days later, on his urging by telephone, I found him in an East End pub, where, in an advanced state of drunkenness, he was surrounded by bums of the first filthy water. He had simply borrowed a bit on the typewriter and bought a couple of bottles of whisky, which he had obviously shared to the last drop with his old "acid-tested" friends, who belonged to a social milieu in which sobriety was distrusted and drunkenness the ideal. He had not one penny piece left. The following morning, armed with several pages of the manuscript, I took Malcolm, bearing the pawnticket, to the pawnbroker. I succeeded in redeeming the "click-clacking conspirator" for the actual amount of twenty-five dollars which had been reluctantly advanced; the pawnbroker refused to take one cent in interest, a rare event in the history of his trade.

Some nights later, we were awakened by loud noises and voices in front of the house. I found that it was Malcolm who, after seeing Mr. Carey, had got drunk with some of his "acid-tested" friends, and they were now in his company, trying to enter by the locked window. I scuffed Malcolm inside, and the others left as fast as their shambling gait would permit; my expletives whipped them on!

As I have inferred, Malcolm's wardrobe was thoroughly depleted. He had one pair of socks, which he washed every night with meticulous care before retiring; the same old sandals, a pair of pants, one faded blue undershirt, and one frayed sports shirt. My sports jacket had grown on him like leaves on a tree. It was the same tweed coat he wore in the photograph that appeared in the February 24, 1947, edition of *Time*; the upturned collar in the portrait reflected his untidiness. In view of the sartorial situation, I gained permission from Mr. Carey to charge at the Bay whatever clothing Malcolm required. Before we left the store he had completely filled his needs; we bought everything but a hat; he never wore one. Much, I am sure, to his embarrassment, when Malcolm turned into our street the children, all of whom adored him, crowded around him and sent out cries of: "Oh looka Malcolm! See all his new do's!"

The successful shopping safari and the happiness derived from it called for a mild celebration. Several neighbours and three of Malcolm's "acid-tested" friends came for the gathering. The latter conducted themselves with the deportment of church elders; one of the guests was a hard-cored policeman who lived across the street, and his presence may have had something to do with their exemplary behaviour. It was Malcolm's habit to slip down to the kitchen for a bedtime snack, and after the party I heard him there, cursing in high gear. I got to the kitchen to find he had carved a couple of wedge-shaped slices of bread and had put between them a thick slice of ham. Somehow, in the preparation, he had also sliced his hand, and the gore from it had saturated the sandwich which, without the turning of a hair, he was devouring with the gusto of the hungriest cannibal!

168

I FOUND LOWRY a person with a hundred facets; at one time when his production slowed, and ideas came even more slowly, he became obsessed with the fervent desire to become a monk. He had discovered a likely monastery during his Mexican sojourn, and asserted that he had communicated with the abbot there, with a view to taking Holy Orders. Later, when buoyancy again possessed him, the monastic kick spent itself; Malcolm dismissed the very thought. "I couldn't stand the short hours of rest, the long hours of labour, the bitter hours of kneeling in prayer without kneepads, the exceedingly short rations and the even shorter haircut. Being the lover of speech that I am, the forced silence would drive me batty — and who wants another crazy monk!"

While we are on the question of whims, it has been said that Malcolm Lowry came to Canada to enlist in World War II. If this were the case, it was just one of the many passing fancies which he enjoyed so much. Although wars and their effects were often discussed, he at no time in my presence suggested putting on any sort of uniform. Firearms made him nervous. "Wars just shouldn't be," he would say.

At times, when he was at a loss for words, our guest would sit alone in his room and ponder his future. Poor Malcolm declared that his life would not be a long one, but, as he phrased it, "a short life with much merriment." Quite often, when I saw him with elbows burrowed firmly into his wobbly knees and chin resting on the platform of his bony knuckles, he would tell me that these silent sessions had to do with eerie spirits and the occult. In the evening he would sometimes stand addressing a corner of the room or, as he put it, "talking to my familiars."

A friend of mine, to whom Malcolm also had become very attached, had for some time been on a steady diet of whisky and bicarbonate of soda; suddenly he made an unscheduled flight into kingdom-come. The abruptness of his demise threw the fear of God into Lowry, and he spoke of it constantly. On the day of the funeral, from the instant we left the house until we returned, Malcolm said not a word. At the funeral chapel he sat alone through the service, with eyes closed tightly, his brows creased in deep concentration. After the final blessing, as we followed the usual custom of viewing the deceased, Malcolm stood with lips opening and sealing again, staring at the emaciated cadaver in abject agony and in such immobility that it seemed as if he too were dead! Still mute until we re-entered the house, he finally broke his silence by saying: "What a delightful way to go!" "Life", he said — and I've thought of it often, "is like a tissue; you use it once and discard it for ever."

Lowry was unpredictable in the extreme. Even under the most ordinary circumstances his whole nature would seem to change, more frequently and notice-ably than with anyone else I have ever known, and when he was under the "ether" his demeanour altered from that of a quiet, suave, gentlemanly, reserved type, to that of a character who might have been raised in the gutter and who used expletives that would have made a longshoreman cringe! Yet never once, drunk or sober, did I hear Malcolm tell an indelicate story; his yarns were always fit for the sitting room.

One day I went out and, returning a couple of hours later, found that Mal-colm had gone out in his brand-new toggery; he had told my wife that a friend from Mexico was in town. We did not hear from him until the following day, when he telephoned to ask if I would see him at a hotel on Pender Street. He asked me to bring down my jacket and his other pair of trousers. An hour later I slammed into the beer parlour. There sat Lowry, drunk, gesticulating impres-sively, with a slopping glass of beer, at the faces of his hangers-on, clothed in no more than an overcoat, underwear and down-at-heel slippers! The rest of his new clothing he had sold.

After the pawning of the typewriter and the disposal of his clothing, I debated whether I should try to make a total abstainer of Malcolm or attempt to control his libations by administering them in small doses. Since he worked better with whisky in his veins, I eventually decided on the latter course. And once, when he had consumed his modest drink before dinner, he remarked: "Brother, you know this is very much like taking Holy Communion — except that these pork chops will taste much more delectable than the wafer symbolizing the dear body of our Lord. How I'd love to drink my fill from the scyphus goblet!" . . . .

(1971)

NOTES ON CONTRIBUTORS

ROBERT B. HEILMAN has been for many years Chairman of the Department of English at the University of Washington. His books of criticism include *Magic in the Web: Action and Language in Othello, This Great Stage: Image and Structure in King Lear* and *Tragedy and Melodrama: Versions of Experience*.

ANTHONY R. KILGALLIN has published articles in many reviews, and is the author of a study of Malcolm Lowry published by Copp Clark of Toronto.

GEORGE WOODCOCK's most recent book is *Canada and the Canadians*. He has completed a critical study of Aldous Huxley which is due to be published in 1972 and is now working on a book on Herbert Read and his philosophical and literary background.

GEOFFREY DURRANT is the author of two recent important studies in Romantic literature, *Wordsworth* in the British Authors series of Cambridge University Press, and *Wordsworth and the Great System*.

DAVID BENHAM taught for a period at the University of Calgary and has now returned to teach in England.

MATTHEW CORRIGAN is a contributor to *Encounter* and other literary magazines.

CONRAD AIKEN, who might be classed as Malcolm Lowry's literary *guru*, is one of the leading living American poets. He has published five novels, more than thirty books of poems, together with volumes of short stories, criticism and autobiography; he was associated with *The Dial* and other historic magazines of the earlier part of the century.

HILDA THOMAS teaches in the Department of English at the University of British Columbia.

The late DOWNIE KIRK was a Vancouver schoolmaster and Malcolm Lowry's close friend during the latter's residence in the Vancouver area.

W. H. NEW is one of the Associate Editors of *Canadian Literature*, has written in many journals on Canadian and Commonwealth writers and writing, and will shortly be publishing his study of Malcolm Lowry in the *Canadian Writers* series. He is at present on a study tour in the Caribbean and England.

PERLE EPSTEIN is the author of *The Private Labyrinth of Malcolm Lowry: Under the Volcano and the Cabbala.* She is a descendant of the celebrated eighteenth century Chassidic teacher, Baal Shem Tov.

WILLIAM MCCONNELL has published many short stories and is himself a publisher who, with his Klanak Press, has introduced to the public a number of significant Canadian writers.

MAURICE J. CAREY was Malcolm Lowry's host in Vancouver for several months during the author's first year in Canada.

SELECTED BIBLIOGRAPHY

1. BOOKS BY MALCOLM LOWRY

Ultramarine. London, 1933.

Under the Volcano. London and New York, 1947.

Hear Us O Lord From Heaven Thy Dwelling Place. London and New York, 1961.

Selected Poems. Edited by Earle Birney and Margerie Lowry. San Francisco, 1962.

Lunar Caustic. Edited by Margerie Lowry and Earle Birney, with Foreword by Conrad Knickerbocker. New York, 1963.

The Selected Letters of Malcolm Lowry. Edited by Harvey Breit and Margerie Lowry. New York, 1965.

Dark as the Grave Wherein My Friend Is Laid. Edited by Douglas Day and Margerie Lowry. New York, 1968.

October Ferry to Gabriola. Edited by Margerie Lowry. New York, 1970.

2. WRITINGS ON MALCOLM LOWRY

(Note: The essays in the present volume are not included.)

Birney, Earle. "Against the Spell of Death," *Prairie Schooner* 37, Winter 1963-64.

———. "Glimpses into the Life of Malcolm Lowry," *Tamarack Review* 19, Spring, 1961.

Bonnefoi, Geneviève. "Souvenir de Quauhnahuac," *Les Lettres Nouvelles,* July-August, 1960.

Costa, Richard Hauer. " 'Ulysses,' Lowry's 'Volcano' and the 'Voyage' between: a study of an unacknowledged literary kinship." *University of Toronto Quarterly,* July, 1967.

Day, Douglas. "Letters of Malcolm Lowry," *Shenandoah Review,* Spring, 1964.

———. "Of Tragic Joy," *Prairie Schooner,* Winter, 1963-64.

Edmonds, Dale. "The short fiction of Malcolm Lowry," *Tulane Studies in English,* 15, 1967.

———. " 'Under the Volcano': a reading of the 'immediate level'," *Tulane Studies in English,* 16, 1968.

Epstein, Perle. *The Private Labyrinth of Malcolm Lowry: Under the Volcano and the Cabbala.* New York, 1969.

Fouchet, Max-Pol. "No se puede . . . " *Lettres Nouvelles*, July-August, 1960.

Françillon, Clarisse. "Malcolm, mon ami," *Lettres Nouvelles*, July-August, 1960.

———. "Souvenirs sur Malcolm Lowry," *Lettres Nouvelles*, November, 1957.

Kilgallin, Anthony R. "Eliot, Joyce and Lowry," *Canadian Author and Bookman*, Winter, 1965.

Knickerbocker, Conrad. "Malcolm Lowry in England," *Paris Review*, Summer, 1966.

———. "The Voyages of Malcolm Lowry," *Prairie Schooner*, Winter, 1963-64.

Magee, A. Peter. "The quest for love," *Emeritus*, Spring, 1965.

Myrer, Anton. "Le Monde au dessous du volcan," *Lettres Nouvelles*, July-August, 1960.

Nadeau, Maurice. "Lowry," *Les Lettres nouvelles*, July-August, 1960.

Spriel, Stephen. "Le Cryptogramme Lowry," *Lettres Nouvelles*, July-August, 1960.

Wild, Bernadette. "Malcolm Lowry: a study of the sea metaphor in 'Under the Volcano'," *University of Windsor Review*, Fall, 1968.

Woodcock, George. "Malcolm Lowry as Novelist," *British Columbia Library Quarterly*, April, 1961.

———. "Malcolm Lowry's 'Under the Volcano'," *Modern Fiction Studies*, Summer, 1958.

———. "On the Day of the Dead," *Northern Review*, December-January, 1953-54.